Presented in Memory of

JAMES P. FAHEY

By

Friends of his brother,
Dr. Paul F. Fahey

PERSONÆ
of EZRA POUND

PERSONÆ

THE COLLECTED SHORTER POEMS OF

EZRA POUND

A NEW DIRECTIONS BOOK

Personae is Ezra Pound's own selection of his shorter poems as made in 1926, with the addition of Appendices I & II, which he added in 1949. His translations of the work of other poets will be found in the separate volumes, *Translations* (1953) and *The Confucian Odes* (1954). His complete early poems including previously unpublished texts, are gathered in *Collected Early Poems* (1976).

CONTENTS

RIPOSTES (1912)

LUSTRA

APPENDIX I

EARLY POEMS, NOT PREVIOUSLY COLLECTED, AND NOW ADDED TO THIS COLLECTION IN 1949, INCLUDING THE POEMS OF T. E. HULME.

THE COMPLETE POETICAL WORKS OF T. E. HULME

APPENDIX II

VERSE OF THE THIRTIES, FIRST PRINTED IN *THE NEW ENGLISH WEEKLY,* AND ADDED TO THIS COLLECTION IN 1949. (PROSE BY A. R. ORAGE.)

PERSONÆ
OF
EZRA POUND

(1908, 1909, 1910)

THE TREE

I STOOD still and was a tree amid the wood,
   Knowing the truth of things unseen before;
   Of Daphne and the laurel bow
And that god-feasting couple old
That grew elm-oak amid the wold.
'Twas not until the gods had been
Kindly entreated, and been brought within
Unto the hearth of their heart's home
That they might do this wonder thing;
Nathless I have been a tree amid the wood
And many a new thing understood
That was rank folly to my head before.

THRENOS

NO more for us the little sighing.
   No more the winds at twilight trouble us.
Lo the fair dead!

No more do I burn.
No more for us the fluttering of wings
That whirred in the air above us.

Lo the fair dead!

No more desire flayeth me,
No more for us the trembling
At the meeting of hands.

Lo the fair dead!

No more for us the wine of the lips,
No more for us the knowledge.

Lo the fair dead!

No more the torrent,
No more for us the meeting-place
(Lo the fair dead!)
Tintagoel.

LA FRAISNE

FOR I was a gaunt, grave councillor
  Being in all things wise, and very old,
  But I have put aside this folly and the cold
That old age weareth for a cloak.

I was quite strong—at least they said so—
The young men at the sword-play;
But I have put aside this folly, being gay
In another fashion that more suiteth me.

I have curled 'mid the boles of the ash wood,
I have hidden my face where the oak
Spread his leaves over me, and the yoke
Of the old ways of men have I cast aside.

By the still pool of Mar-nan-otha
Have I found me a bride
That was a dog-wood tree some syne.
She hath called me from mine old ways
She hath hushed my rancour of council,
Bidding me praise

Naught but the wind that flutters in the leaves.

She hath drawn me from mine old ways,
Till men say that I am mad;
But I have seen the sorrow of men, and am glad,
For I know that the wailing and bitterness are a
    folly.
And I? I have put aside all folly and all grief.
I wrapped my tears in an ellum leaf
And left them under a stone
And now men call me mad because I have thrown
All folly from me, putting it aside
To leave the old barren ways of men,

Because my bride
Is a pool of the wood, and
Though all men say that I am mad
It is only that I am glad,
Very glad, for my bride hath toward me a great love
That is sweeter than the love of women
That plague and burn and drive one away.

Aie-e! 'Tis true that I am gay
  Quite gay, for I have her alone here
  And no man troubleth us.

Once when I was among the young men . . .
And they said I was quite strong, among the young
      men.
Once there was a woman . . .
. . . but I forget . . . she was . .
. . . I hope she will not come again.

. . . I do not remember . . . . .

I think she hurt me once, but . .
That was very long ago.

I do not like to remember things any more.

I like one little band of winds that blow
In the ash trees here:
For we are quite alone
Here 'mid the ash trees.

CINO

BAH! I have sung women in three cities,
But it is all the same;
And I will sing of the sun.

Lips, words, and you snare them,
Dreams, words, and they are as jewels,
Strange spells of old deity,
Ravens, nights, allurement:
And they are not;
Having become the souls of song.

Eyes, dreams, lips, and the night goes.
Being upon the road once more,
They are not.
Forgetful in their towers of our tuneing
Once for wind-runeing
They dream us-toward and
Sighing, say, "Would Cino,
Passionate Cino, of the wrinkling eyes,
Gay Cino, of quick laughter,
Cino, of the dare, the jibe,
Frail Cino, strongest of his tribe
That tramp old ways beneath the sun-light,
Would Cino of the Luth were here!"

Once, twice, a year—
Vaguely thus word they:

>   "Cino?" "Oh, eh, Cino Polnesi
>   The singer is't you mean?"
>   "Ah yes, passed once our way,
>   A saucy fellow, but . . .
>   (Oh they are all one these vagabonds),
>   Peste! 'tis his own songs?
>   Or some other's that he sings?
>   But *you,* My Lord, how with your city?"

But you "My Lord," God's pity!
And all I knew were out, My Lord, you
Were Lack-land Cino, e'en as I am,
O Sinistro.

I have sung women in three cities.
But it is all one.
I will sing of the sun.
. . . eh? . . . they mostly had grey eyes,
But it is all one, I will sing of the sun.

> " 'Pollo Phoibee, old tin pan, you
> Glory to Zeus' aegis-day,
> Shield o' steel-blue, th' heaven o'er us
> Hath for boss thy lustre gay!
>
> 'Pollo Phoibee, to our way-fare
> Make thy laugh our wander-lied;
> Bid thy 'fulgence bear away care.
> Cloud and rain-tears pass they fleet!
>
> Seeking e'er the new-laid rast-way
> To the gardens of the sun . . .
>
> .   .   .   .   .   .
>
> I have sung women in three cities
> But it is all one.
>
> I will sing of the white birds
> In the blue waters of heaven,
> The clouds that are spray to its sea."

NA AUDIART

Que be-m vols mal

NOTE: Anyone who has read anything of the troubadours knows well the tale of Bertran of Born and My Lady Maent of Montagnac, and knows also the song he made when she would none of him, the song wherein he, seeking to find or make her equal, begs of each preëminent lady of Langue d'Oc some trait or some fair semblance: thus of Cembelins her "esgart amoros" to wit, her love-lit glance, of Aelis her speech free-running, of the Vicomtess of Chalais her throat and her two hands, at Roacoart of Anhes her hair golden as Iseult's; and even in this fashion of Lady Audiart "although she would that ill come unto him" he sought and praised the lineaments of the torse. And all this to make "Una dompna soiseubuda" a borrowed lady or as the Italians translated it "Una donna ideale."

THOUGH thou well dost wish me ill
            Audiart, Audiart,
   Where thy bodice laces start
As ivy fingers clutching through
Its crevices,

            Audiart, Audiart,
Stately, tall and lovely tender
Who shall render

            Audiart, Audiart,
Praises meet unto thy fashion?
Here a word kiss!

            Pass I on
Unto Lady "Miels-de-Ben,"
Having praised thy girdle's scope
How the stays ply back from it;
I breathe no hope
That thou shouldst . . .

            Nay no whit
Bespeak thyself for anything.
Just a word in thy praise, girl,
Just for the swirl
Thy satins make upon the stair,
'Cause never a flaw was there
Where thy torse and limbs are met
Though thou hate me, read it set

In rose and gold.[1]
Or when the minstrel, tale half told,
Shall burst to lilting at the praise
                    "Audiart, Audiart" . . .
Bertrans, master of his lays,
Bertrans of Aultaforte thy praise
Sets forth, and though thou hate me well,
Yea though thou wish me ill,
                    Audiart, Audiart.
Thy loveliness is here writ till,
                    Audiart,
Oh, till thou come again.[2]
And being bent and wrinkled, in a form
That hath no perfect limning, when the warm
Youth dew is cold
Upon thy hands, and thy old soul
Scorning a new, wry'd casement,
Churlish at seemed misplacement,
Finds the earth as bitter
As now seems it sweet,
Being so young and fair
As then only in dreams,
Being then young and wry'd,
Broken of ancient pride,
Thou shalt then soften,
Knowing, I know not how,
Thou wert once she
                    Audiart, Audiart
For whose fairness one forgave
                    Audiart,
Audiart
          Que be-m vols mal.

---

[1] *I.e.* in illumed manuscript.
[2] Reincarnate.

VILLONAUD FOR THIS YULE

TOWARDS the Noel that morte saison
  (*Christ make the shepherds' homage dear!*)
  Then when the grey wolves everychone
Drink of the winds their chill small-beer
And lap o' the snows food's gueredon
Then makyth my heart his yule-tide cheer
(Skoal! with the dregs if the clear be gone!)
Wining the ghosts of yester-year.

Ask ye what ghosts I dream upon?
(*What of the magians' scented gear?*)
The ghosts of dead loves everyone
That make the stark winds reek with fear
Lest love return with the foison sun
And slay the memories that me cheer
(Such as I drink to mine fashion)
Wining the ghosts of yester-year.

Where are the joys my heart had won?
(*Saturn and Mars to Zeus drawn near!*)[1]
Where are the lips mine lay upon,
Aye! where are the glances feat and clear
That bade my heart his valour don?
I skoal to the eyes as grey-blown mere
(Who knows whose was that paragon?)
Wining the ghosts of yester-year.

Prince: ask me not what I have done
Nor what God hath that can me cheer
But ye ask first where the winds are gone
Wining the ghosts of yester-year.

[1] *Signum Nativitatis.*

A VILLONAUD: BALLAD OF THE GIBBET

OR THE SONG OF THE SIXTH COMPANION

SCENE: *"En ce bourdel où tenons nostre estat."*

It being remembered that there were six of us with Master Villon, when that expecting presently to be hanged he writ a ballad whereof ye know:

"Frères humains qui après nous vivez."

D RINK ye a skoal for the gallows tree!
François and Margot and thee and me,
Drink we the comrades merrily
That said us, "Till then" for the gallows tree!

Fat Pierre with the hook gauche-main,
Thomas Larron "Ear-the-less,"
Tybalde and that armouress
Who gave this poignard its premier stain
Pinning the Guise that had been fain
To make him a mate of the "Haulte Noblesse"
And bade her be out with ill address
As a fool that mocketh his drue's disdeign.

Drink we a skoal for the gallows tree!
François and Margot and thee and me,
Drink we to Marienne Ydole,
That hell brenn not her o'er cruelly.

Drink we the lusty robbers twain,
Black is the pitch o' their wedding dress,[1]
Lips shrunk back for the wind's caress
As lips shrink back when we feel the strain
Of love that loveth in hell's disdeign,
And sense the teeth through the lips that press
'Gainst our lips for the soul's distress
That striveth to ours across the pain.

---

[1] Certain gibbeted corpses used to be coated with tar as a preservative; thus one scarecrow served as warning for considerable time. See Hugo, *L'Homme qui Rit.*

Drink we skoal to the gallows tree!
François and Margot and thee and me,
For Jehan and Raoul de Vallerie
Whose frames have the night and its winds in fee.

Maturin, Guillaume, Jacques d'Allmain,
Culdou lacking a coat to bless
One lean moiety of his nakedness
That plundered St. Hubert back o' the fane:
Aie! the lean bare tree is widowed again
For Michault le Borgne that would confess
In "faith and troth" to a traitoress,
"Which of his brothers had he slain?"

But drink we skoal to the gallows tree!
François and Margot and thee and me:

These that we loved shall God love less
And smite always at their faibleness?

Skoal!! to the gallows! and then pray we:
God damn his hell out speedily
And bring their souls to his "Haulte Citee."

MESMERISM

"And a cat's in the water-butt."—ROBERT BROWNING

AYE you're a man that! ye old mesmerizer
   Tyin' your meanin' in seventy swadelin's,
   One must of needs be a hang'd early riser
To catch you at worm turning. Holy Odd's body-
    kins!

"Cat's i' the water butt!" Thought's in your verse-
    barrel,
Tell us this thing rather, then we'll believe you,
You, Master Bob Browning, spite your apparel
Jump to your sense and give praise as we'd lief do.

You wheeze as a head-cold long-tonsilled Calliope,
But God! what a sight you ha' got o' our in'ards,
Mad as a hatter but surely no Myope,
Broad as all ocean and leanin' man-kin'ards.

Heart that was big as the bowels of Vesuvius,
Words that were wing'd as her sparks in eruption,
Eagled and thundered as Jupiter Pluvius,
Sound in your wind past all signs o' corruption.

Here's to you, Old Hippety-Hop o' the accents,
True to the Truth's sake and crafty dissector,
You grabbed at the gold sure; had no need to pack
    cents
Into your versicles.
            Clear sight's elector!

FAMAM LIBROSQUE CANO

YOUR songs?
                    Oh! The little mothers
          Will sing them in the twilight,
And when the night
Shrinketh the kiss of the dawn
That loves and kills,
What times the swallow fills
Her note, the little rabbit folk
That some call children,
Such as are up and wide,
Will laugh your verses to each other,
Pulling on their shoes for the day's business,
Serious child business that the world
Laughs at, and grows stale;
Such is the tale
—Part of it—of thy song-life.

Mine?

          A book is known by them that read
          That same. Thy public in my screed
          Is listed. Well! Some score years hence
          Behold mine audience,
          As we had seen him yesterday.

          Scrawny, be-spectacled, out at heels,
Such an one as the world feels
A sort of curse against its guzzling
And its age-lasting wallow for red greed
And yet; full speed
Though it should run for its own getting,
Will turn aside to sneer at
'Cause he hath
No coin, no will to snatch the aftermath
Of Mammon

Such an one as women draw away from
For the tobacco ashes scattered on his coat
And sith his throat
Shows razor's unfamiliarity
And three days' beard;

Such an one picking a ragged
Backless copy from the stall,
Too cheap for cataloguing,
Loquitur,

    "Ah-eh! the strange rare name . . .
Ah-eh! He must be rare if even *I* have not . . ."
And lost mid-page
Such age
As his pardons the habit,
He analyses form and thought to see
How I 'scaped immortality.

PRAISE OF YSOLT

IN vain have I striven,
        to teach my heart to bow;
  In vain have I said to him
"There be many singers greater than thou."

But his answer cometh, as winds and as lutany,
As a vague crying upon the night
That leaveth me no rest, saying ever,
        "Song, a song."

Their echoes play upon each other in the twilight
Seeking ever a song.
Lo, I am worn with travail
And the wandering of many roads hath made my
       eyes
As dark red circles filled with dust.
Yet there is a trembling upon me in the twilight,
     And little red elf words crying "A song,"
     Little grey elf words crying for a song,
     Little brown leaf words crying "A song,"
     Little green leaf words crying for a song.
The words are as leaves, old brown leaves in the
       spring time
Blowing they know not whither, seeking a song.

White words as snow flakes but they are cold,
Moss words, lip words, words of slow streams.

In vain have I striven
        to teach my soul to bow,
In vain have I pled with him:
     "There be greater souls than thou."

For in the morn of my years there came a woman
As moonlight calling,
As the moon calleth the tides,
        "Song, a song."

Wherefore I made her a song and she went from me
As the moon doth from the sea,
But still came the leaf words, little brown elf words
Saying "The soul sendeth us."
                    "A song, a song!"
And in vain I cried unto them "I have no song
For she I sang of hath gone from me."

But my soul sent a woman, a woman of the wonder-
            folk,
A woman as fire upon the pine woods
            crying "Song, a song."
As the flame crieth unto the sap.
My song was ablaze with her and she went from me
As flame leaveth the embers so went she unto new
            forests
And the words were with me
            crying ever "Song, a song."

And I "I have no song,"
Till my soul sent a woman as the sun:
Yea as the sun calleth to the seed,
As the spring upon the bough
So is she that cometh, the mother of songs,
She that holdeth the wonder words within her eyes
The words, little elf words
            that call ever unto me,
                    "Song, a song."

In vain have I striven with my soul
            to teach my soul to bow.
What soul boweth
            while in his heart art thou?

DE AEGYPTO

EVEN I, am he who knoweth the roads
Through the sky, and the wind thereof is my
    body.

I have beheld the Lady of Life,
I, even I, who fly with the swallows.

Green and gray is her raiment,
Trailing along the wind.

I, even I, am he who knoweth the roads
Through the sky, and the wind thereof is my body.

Manus animam pinxit,
My pen is in my hand

To write the acceptable word. . . .
My mouth to chant the pure singing!

Who hath the mouth to receive it,
The song of the Lotus of Kumi?

I, even I, am he who knoweth the roads
Through the sky, and the wind thereof is my body.

I am flame that riseth in the sun,
I, even I, who fly with the swallows.

The moon is upon my forehead,
The winds are under my lips.

The moon is a great pearl in the waters of sapphire,
Cool to my fingers the flowing waters.

I, even I, am he who knoweth the roads
Through the sky, and the wind thereof is my body.

FOR E. McC.

That was my counter-blade under Leonardo Terrone, Master of Fence

GONE while your tastes were keen to you,
Gone where the grey winds call to you,
    By that high fencer, even Death,
Struck of the blade that no man parrieth;
Such is your fence, one saith,
    One that hath known you.
Drew you your sword most gallantly
Made you your pass most valiantly
    'Gainst that grey fencer, even Death.

Gone as a gust of breath
Faith! no man tarrieth,
"Se il cor ti manca," but it failed thee not!
"Non ti fidar," it is the sword that speaks
"In me." [1]

Thou trusted'st in thyself and met the blade
'Thout mask or gauntlet, and art laid
As memorable broken blades that be
Kept as bold trophies of old pageantry.
As old Toledos past their days of war
Are kept mnemonic of the strokes they bore,
So art thou with us, being good to keep
In our heart's sword-rack, though thy sword-arm
    sleep.

ENVOI

Struck of the blade that no man parrieth
Pierced of the point that toucheth lastly all,
'Gainst that grey fencer, even Death,
Behold the shield! He shall not take thee all.

[1] Sword-rune "If thy heart fail thee trust not in me."

IN DURANCE

(1907)

I AM homesick after mine own kind,
Oh I know that there are folk about me,
   friendly faces,
But I am homesick after mine own kind.

"These sell our pictures"! Oh well,
They reach me not, touch me some edge or that,
But reach me not and all my life's become
One flame, that reaches not beyond
My heart's own hearth,
Or hides among the ashes there for thee.
"Thee"? Oh, "Thee" is who cometh first
Out of mine own soul-kin,
For I am homesick after mine own kind
And ordinary people touch me not.
                And I am homesick
After mine own kind that know, and feel
And have some breath for beauty and the arts.

Aye, I am wistful for my kin of the spirit
And have none about me save in the shadows
When come *they,* surging of power, "DAEMON,"
"Quasi KALOUN." S.T. says Beauty is most that, a
    "calling to the soul."
Well then, so call they, the swirlers out of the mist
    of my soul,
They that come mewards, bearing old magic.

But for all that, I am homesick after mine own kind
And would meet kindred even as I am,
Flesh-shrouded bearing the secret.
"All they that with strange sadness"
Have the earth in mockery, and are kind to all,
My fellows, aye I know the glory

Of th' unbounded ones, but ye, that hide
As I hide most the while
And burst forth to the windows only whiles or whiles
For love, or hope, or beauty or for power,
Then smoulder, with the lids half closed
And are untouched by echoes of the world.

Oh ye, my fellows: with the seas between us some be,
Purple and sapphire for the silver shafts
Of sun and spray all shattered at the bows;
And some the hills hold off,
The little hills to east of us, though here we
Have damp and plain to be our shutting in.

And yet my soul sings "Up!" and we are one.
Yea thou, and Thou, and THOU, and all my kin
To whom my breast and arms are ever warm,
For that I love ye as the wind the trees
That holds their blossoms and their leaves in cure
And calls the utmost singing from the boughs
That 'thout him, save the aspen, were as dumb
Still shade, and bade no whisper speak the birds of
      how
"Beyond, beyond, beyond, there lies . . ."

MARVOIL

A POOR clerk I, "Arnaut the less" they call me,
   And because I have small mind to sit
   Day long, long day cooped on a stool
A-jumbling o' figures for Maître Jacques Polin,
I ha' taken to rambling the South here.

The Vicomte of Beziers 's not such a bad lot.
I made rimes to his lady this three year:
Vers and canzone, till that damn'd son of Aragon,
Alfonso the half-bald, took to hanging
His helmet at Beziers.
Then came what might come, to wit: three men and
      one woman,
Beziers off at Mont-Ausier, I and his lady
Singing the stars in the turrets of Beziers,
And one lean Aragonese cursing the seneschal
To the end that you see, friends:

Aragon   cursing   in   Aragon,   Beziers   busy   at
      Beziers—
Bored to an inch of extinction,
Tibors all tongue and temper at Mont-Ausier,
Me! in this damn'd inn of Avignon,
Stringing long verse for the Burlatz;
All   for   one   half-bald,   knock-knee'd   king   of   the
      Aragonese,
Alfonso, Quattro, poke-nose.

And if when I am dead
They take the trouble to tear out this wall here,
They'll know more of Arnaut of Marvoil
Than half his canzoni say of him.
As for will and testament I leave none,
Save this: "Vers and canzone to the Countess of
      Beziers

In return for the first kiss she gave me."
May her eyes and her cheek be fair
To all men except the King of Aragon,
And may I come speedily to Beziers
Whither my desire and my dream have preceded me.

O hole in the wall here! be thou my jongleur
As ne'er had I other, and when the wind blows,
Sing thou the grace of the Lady of Beziers,
For even as thou art hollow before I fill thee with
    this parchment,
So is my heart hollow when she filleth not mine eyes,
And so were my mind hollow, did she not fill utterly
    my thought.

Wherefore, O hole in the wall here,
When the wind blows sigh thou for my sorrow
That I have not the Countess of Beziers
Close in my arms here.
Even as thou shalt soon have this parchment.

O hole in the wall here, be thou my jongleur,
And though thou sighest my sorrow in the wind,
Keep yet my secret in thy breast here;
Even as I keep her image in my heart here.

Mihi pergamena deest

AND THUS IN NINEVEH

" AYE! I am a poet and upon my tomb
Shall maidens scatter rose leaves
And men myrtles, ere the night
Slays day with her dark sword.

"Lo! this thing is not mine
Nor thine to hinder,
For the custom is full old,
And here in Nineveh have I beheld
Many a singer pass and take his place
In those dim halls where no man troubleth
His sleep or song.
And many a one hath sung his songs
More craftily, more subtle-souled than I;
And many a one now doth surpass
My wave-worn beauty with his wind of flowers,
Yet am I poet, and upon my tomb
Shall all men scatter rose leaves
Ere the night slay light
With her blue sword.

"It is not, Raana, that my song rings highest
Or more sweet in tone than any, but that I
Am here a Poet, that doth drink of life
As lesser men drink wine."

THE WHITE STAG

I HA' seen them 'mid the clouds on the heather.
Lo! they pause not for love nor for sorrow,
Yet their eyes are as the eyes of a maid to her
    lover,
When the white hart breaks his cover
And the white wind breaks the morn.

> *"'Tis the white stag, Fame, we're a-hunting,*
> *Bid the world's hounds come to horn!"*

GUIDO INVITES YOU THUS [1]

" LAPPO I leave behind and Dante too,
    Lo, I would sail the seas with thee alone!
    Talk me no love talk, no bought-cheap
fiddl'ry,
Mine is the ship and thine the merchandise,
All the blind earth knows not th'emprise
Whereto thou calledst and whereto I call.

Lo, I have seen thee bound about with dreams,
Lo, I have known thy heart and its desire;
Life, all of it, my sea, and all men's streams
Are fused in it as flames of an altar fire!
Lo, thou hast voyaged not! The ship is mine."

[1] The reference is to Dante's sonnet "Guido vorrei . . . "

25

NIGHT LITANY

O DIEU, purifiez nos cœurs!
          Purifiez nos cœurs!

Yea the lines hast thou laid unto me
          in pleasant places,
And the beauty of this thy Venice
          hast thou shown unto me
Until is its loveliness become unto me
          a thing of tears.

O God, what great kindness
          have we done in times past
          and forgotten it,
That thou givest this wonder unto us,
          O God of waters?

O God of the night,
          What great sorrow
Cometh unto us,
          That thou thus repayest us
Before the time of its coming?

O God of silence,
          Purifiez nos cœurs,
          Purifiez nos cœurs,
For we have seen
The glory of the shadow of the
          likeness of thine handmaid,

Yea, the glory of the shadow
          of thy Beauty hath walked
Upon the shadow of the waters
In this thy Venice.
          And before the holiness

Of the shadow of thy handmaid
   Have I hidden mine eyes,
         O God of waters.

O God of silence,
         Purifiez nos cœurs,
         Purifiez nos cœurs,
O God of waters,
         make clean our hearts within us,
         For I have seen the
Shadow of this thy Venice
Floating upon the waters,
         And thy stars

Have seen this thing, out of their far courses
Have they seen this thing,
         O God of waters,
Even as are thy stars
Silent unto us in their far-coursing,
Even so is mine heart
         become silent within me.

         Purifiez nos cœurs
O God of the silence,
         Purifiez nos cœurs
O God of waters.

SESTINA: ALTAFORTE

Loquitur: *En* Bertrans de Born.
  Dante Alighieri put this man in hell for that he was a stirrer
  up of strife.
  Eccovi!
  Judge ye!
  Have I dug him up again?
The scene is at his castle, Altaforte. "Papiols" is his jongleur.
"The Leopard," the *device* of Richard Cœur de Lion.

I

DAMN it all! all this our South stinks peace.
    You whoreson dog, Papiols, come! Let's to
        music!
I have no life save when the swords clash.
But ah! when I see the standards gold, vair, purple,
        opposing
And the broad fields beneath them turn crimson,
Then howl I my heart nigh mad with rejoicing.

II

In hot summer have I great rejoicing
When the tempests kill the earth's foul peace,
And the lightnings from black heav'n flash crimson,
And the fierce thunders roar me their music
And the winds shriek through the clouds mad,
        opposing,
And through all the riven skies God's swords clash.

III

Hell grant soon we hear again the swords clash!
And the shrill neighs of destriers in battle rejoicing,
Spiked breast to spiked breast opposing!
Better one hour's stour than a year's peace
With fat boards, bawds, wine and frail music!
Bah! there's no wine like the blood's crimson!

IV

And I love to see the sun rise blood-crimson.
And I watch his spears through the dark clash
And it fills all my heart with rejoicing
And pries wide my mouth with fast music
When I see him so scorn and defy peace,
His lone might 'gainst all darkness opposing.

V

The man who fears war and squats opposing
My words for stour, hath no blood of crimson
But is fit only to rot in womanish peace
Far from where worth's won and the swords clash
For the death of such sluts I go rejoicing;
Yea, I fill all the air with my music.

VI

Papiols, Papiols, to the music!
There's no sound like to swords swords opposing,
No cry like the battle's rejoicing
When our elbows and swords drip the crimson
And our charges 'gainst "The Leopard's" rush
    clash.
May God damn for ever all who cry "Peace!"

VII

And let the music of the swords make them crimson!
Hell grant soon we hear again the swords clash!
Hell blot black for alway the thought "Peace"!

PIERE VIDAL OLD

It is of Piere Vidal, the fool *par excellence* of all Provence, of whom the tale tells how he ran mad, as a wolf, because of his love for Loba of Penautier, and how men hunted him with dogs through the mountains of Cabaret and brought him for dead to the dwelling of this Loba (she-wolf) of Penautier, and how she and her Lord had him healed and made welcome, and he stayed some time at that court. He speaks:

WHEN I but think upon the great dead days
  And turn my mind upon that splendid
      madness,
Lo! I do curse my strength
And blame the sun his gladness;
For that the one is dead
And the red sun mocks my sadness.

Behold me, Vidal, that was fool of fools!
Swift as the king wolf was I and as strong
When tall stags fled me through the alder brakes,
And every jongleur knew me in his song,
And the hounds fled and the deer fled
And none fled over-long.

Even the grey pack knew me and knew fear.
God! how the swiftest hind's blood spurted hot
Over the sharpened teeth and purpling lips!
Hot was that hind's blood yet it scorched me not
As did first scorn, then lips of the Penautier!
Aye ye are fools, if ye think time can blot

From Piere Vidal's remembrance that blue night.
God! but the purple of the sky was deep!
Clear, deep, translucent, so the stars me seemed
Set deep in crystal; and because my sleep
—Rare visitor—came not,—the Saints I guerdon
For that restlessness—Piere set to keep

One more fool's vigil with the hollyhocks.
Swift came the Loba, as a branch that's caught,
Torn, green and silent in the swollen Rhone,
Green was her mantle, close, and wrought
Of some thin silk stuff that's scarce stuff at all,
But like a mist wherethrough her white form fought,

And conquered! Ah God! conquered!
Silent my mate came as the night was still.
Speech? Words? Faugh! Who talks of words
    and love?!
Hot is such love and silent,
Silent as fate is, and as strong until
It faints in taking and in giving all.

Stark, keen, triumphant, till it plays at death.
God! she was white then, splendid as some tomb
High wrought of marble, and the panting breath
Ceased utterly. Well, then I waited, drew,
Half-sheathed, then naked from its saffron sheath
Drew full this dagger that doth tremble here.

Just then she woke and mocked the less keen blade.
Ah God, the Loba! and my only mate!
Was there such flesh made ever and unmade!
God curse the years that turn such women grey!
Behold here Vidal, that was hunted, flayed,
Shamed and yet bowed not and that won at last.

And yet I curse the sun for his red gladness,
I that have known strath, garth, brake, dale,
And every run-away of the wood through that great
    madness,
Behold me shrivelled as an old oak's trunk
And made men's mock'ry in my rotten sadness!

No man hath heard the glory of my days:
No man hath dared and won his dare as I:
One night, one body and one welding flame!
What do ye own, ye niggards! that can buy
Such glory of the earth? Or who will win
Such battle-guerdon with his "prowesse high"?

O Age gone lax! O stunted followers,
That mask at passions and desire desires,
Behold me shrivelled, and your mock of mocks;
And yet I mock you by the mighty fires
That burnt me to this ash.

.   .   .   .

Ah! Cabaret! Ah Cabaret, thy hills again!

.   .   .   .

Take your hands off me! . . .   [*Sniffing the air.*
                    Ha! this scent is hot!

PARACELSUS IN EXCELSIS

"**B**EING no longer human, why should I
          Pretend humanity or don the frail attire?
          Men have I known and men, but never one
Was grown so free an essence, or become
So simply element as what I am.
The mist goes from the mirror and I see.
Behold! the world of forms is swept beneath—
Turmoil grown visible beneath our peace,
And we that are grown formless, rise above—
Fluids intangible that have been men,
We seem as statues round whose high-risen base
Some overflowing river is run mad,
In us alone the element of calm."

BALLAD OF THE GOODLY FERE

Simon Zelotes speaketh it somewhile after the Crucifixion

Fere = Mate, Companion.

HA' we lost the goodliest fere o' all
    For the priests and the gallows tree?
    Aye lover he was of brawny men,
O' ships and the open sea.

When they came wi' a host to take Our Man
His smile was good to see,
"First let these go!" quo' our Goodly Fere,
"Or I'll see ye damned," says he.

Aye he sent us out through the crossed high spears
And the scorn of his laugh rang free,
"Why took ye not me when I walked about
Alone in the town?" says he.

Oh we drunk his "Hale" in the good red wine
When we last made company,
No capon priest was the Goodly Fere
But a man o' men was he.

I ha' seen him drive a hundred men
Wi' a bundle o' cords swung free,
That they took the high and holy house
For their pawn and treasury.

They'll no' get him a' in a book I think
Though they write it cunningly;
No mouse of the scrolls was the Goodly Fere
But aye loved the open sea.

If they think they ha' snared our Goodly Fere
They are fools to the last degree.
"I'll go to the feast," quo' our Goodly Fere,
"Though I go to the gallows tree."

"Ye ha' seen me heal the lame and blind,
And wake the dead," says he,
"Ye shall see one thing to master all:
'Tis how a brave man dies on the tree."

A son of God was the Goodly Fere
That bade us his brothers be.
I ha' seen him cow a thousand men.
I have seen him upon the tree.

He cried no cry when they drave the nails
And the blood gushed hot and free,
The hounds of the crimson sky gave tongue
But never a cry cried he.

I ha' seen him cow a thousand men
On the hills o' Galilee,
They whined as he walked out calm between,
Wi' his eyes like the grey o' the sea,

Like the sea that brooks no voyaging
With the winds unleashed and free,
Like the sea that he cowed at Genseret
Wi' twey words spoke' suddently.

A master of men was the Goodly Fere,
A mate of the wind and sea,
If they think they ha' slain our Goodly Fere
They are fools eternally.

I ha' seen him eat o' the honey-comb
Sin' they nailed him to the tree.

ON HIS OWN FACE IN A GLASS

O STRANGE face there in the glass!
    O ribald company, O saintly host,
    O sorrow-swept my fool,
What answer? O ye myriad
That strive and play and pass,
Jest, challenge, counterlie!
I? I? I?

        And ye?

THE EYES

R EST Master, for we be a-weary, weary
    And would feel the fingers of the wind
    Upon these lids that lie over us
Sodden and lead-heavy.

    Rest brother, for lo! the dawn is without!
The yellow flame paleth
And the wax runs low.

Free us, for without be goodly colours,
Green of the wood-moss and flower colours,
And coolness beneath the trees.

    Free us, for we perish
In this ever-flowing monotony
Of ugly print marks, black
Upon white parchment.

    Free us, for there is one
Whose smile more availeth
Than all the age-old knowledge of thy books:
And we would look thereon.

FRANCESCA

Y OU came in out of the night
And there were flowers in your hands,
Now you will come out of a confusion of
people,
Out of a turmoil of speech about you.

I who have seen you amid the primal things
Was angry when they spoke your name
In ordinary places.
I would that the cool waves might flow over my
mind,
And that the world should dry as a dead leaf,
Or as a dandelion seed-pod and be swept away,
So that I might find you again,
Alone.

PLANH FOR THE YOUNG ENGLISH
KING

*That is, Prince Henry Plantagenet, elder brother to Richard
Cœur de Lion.*
From the Provençal of Bertrans de Born "Si tuit li dolh elh
plor elh marrimen."

I F all the grief and woe and bitterness,
All dolour, ill and every evil chance
That ever came upon this grieving world
Were set together they would seem but light
Against the death of the young English King.
Worth lieth riven and Youth dolorous,
The world o'ershadowed, soiled and overcast,
Void of all joy and full of ire and sadness.

Grieving and sad and full of bitterness
Are left in teen the liegemen courteous.
The joglars supple and the troubadours.

O'er much hath ta'en Sir Death that deadly warrior
In taking from them the young English King,
Who made the freest hand seem covetous.
'Las! Never was nor will be in this world
The balance for this loss in ire and sadness!

O skillful Death and full of bitterness,
Well mayst thou boast that thou the best chevalier
That any folk e'er had, hast from us taken;
Sith nothing is that unto worth pertaineth
But had its life in the young English King
And better were it, should God grant his pleasure,
That he should live than many a living dastard
That doth but wound the good with ire and sadness.

From this faint world, how full of bitterness
Love takes his way and holds his joy deceitful,
Sith no thing is but turneth unto anguish
And each to-day 'vails less than yestere'en,
Let each man visage this young English King
That was most valiant 'mid all worthiest men!
Gone is his body fine and amorous,
Whence have we grief, discord and deepest sadness.

Him, whom it pleased for our great bitterness
To come to earth to draw us from misventure,
Who drank of death for our salvacioun,
Him do we pray as to a Lord most righteous
And humble eke, that the young English King
He please to pardon, as true pardon is,
And bid go in with honourèd companions
There where there is no grief, nor shall be sadness.

BALLATETTA

THE light became her grace and dwelt among
Blind eyes and shadows that are formed as
men;
Lo, how the light doth melt us into song:

The broken sunlight for a helm she beareth
Who hath my heart in jurisdiction.
In wild-wood never fawn nor fallow fareth
So silent light; no gossamer is spun
So delicate as she is, when the sun
Drives the clear emeralds from the bended grasses
Lest they should parch too swiftly, where she passes.

PRAYER FOR HIS LADY'S LIFE
FROM PROPERTIUS, ELEGIAE, LIB. III, 26

HERE let thy clemency, Persephone, hold firm,
Do thou, Pluto, bring here no greater
harshness.
So many thousand beauties are gone down to
Avernus,
Ye might let one remain above with us.

With you is Iope, with you the white-gleaming Tyro,
With you is Europa and the shameless Pasiphae,
And all the fair from Troy and all from Achaia,
From the sundered realms, of Thebes and of aged
Priamus;
And all the maidens of Rome, as many as they were,
They died and the greed of your flame consumes
them.

Here let thy clemency, Persephone, hold firm,
Do thou, Pluto, bring here no greater harshness.
So many thousand fair are gone down to Avernus,
Ye might let one remain above with us.

SPEECH FOR PSYCHE IN THE GOLDEN
BOOK OF APULEIUS

ALL night, and as the wind lieth among
    The cypress trees, he lay,
    Nor held me save as air that brusheth by one
Close, and as the petals of flowers in falling
Waver and seem not drawn to earth, so he
Seemed over me to hover light as leaves
And closer me than air,
And music flowing through me seemed to open
Mine eyes upon new colours.
O winds, what wind can match the weight of him!

"BLANDULA, TENELLA, VAGULA"

WHAT hast thou, O my soul, with paradise?
    Will we not rather, when our freedom's
      won,
Get us to some clear place wherein the sun
Lets drift in on us through the olive leaves
A liquid glory? If at Sirmio,
My soul, I meet thee, when this life's outrun,
Will we not find some headland consecrated
By aery apostles of terrene delight,
Will not our cult be founded on the waves,
Clear sapphire, cobalt, cyanine,
On triune azures, the impalpable
Mirrors unstill of the eternal change?

Soul, if She meet us there, will any rumour
Of havens more high and courts desirable
Lure us beyond the cloudy peak of Riva?

ERAT HORA

"THANK you, whatever comes." And then
        she turned
        And, as the ray of sun on hanging flowers
Fades when the wind hath lifted them aside,
Went swiftly from me. Nay, whatever comes
One hour was sunlit and the most high gods
May not make boast of any better thing
Than to have watched that hour as it passed.

ROME

FROM THE FRENCH OF JOACHIM DU BELLAY

"Troica Roma resurges."—PROPERTIUS

O THOU new comer who seek'st Rome in
        Rome
        And find'st in Rome no thing thou canst call
        Roman;
Arches worn old and palaces made common,
Rome's name alone within these walls keeps home.

Behold how pride and ruin can befall
One who hath set the whole world 'neath her laws,
All-conquering, now conquerèd, because
She is Time's prey and Time consumeth all.

Rome that art Rome's one sole last monument,
Rome that alone hast conquered Rome the town,
Tiber alone, transient and seaward bent,
Remains of Rome. O world, thou unconstant mime!
That which stands firm in thee Time batters down,
And that which fleeteth doth outrun swift time.

HER MONUMENT, THE IMAGE CUT THEREON

FROM THE ITALIAN OF LEOPARDI

SUCH wast thou,
  Who art now
    But buried dust and rusted skeleton.
Above the bones and mire,
Motionless, placed in vain,
Mute mirror of the flight of speeding years,
Sole guard of grief
Sole guard of memory
Standeth this image of the beauty sped.

O glance, when thou wast still as thou art now,
How hast thou set the fire
A-tremble in men's veins; O lip curved high
To mind me of some urn of full delight,
O throat girt round of old with swift desire,
O palms of Love, that in your wonted ways
Not once but many a day
Felt hands turn ice a-sudden, touching ye,
That ye were once! of all the grace ye had
That which remaineth now
Shameful, most sad
Finds 'neath this rock fit mould, fit resting place!

And still when fate recalleth,
Even that semblance that appears amongst us
Is like to heaven's most 'live imagining.
All, all our life's eternal mystery!
To-day, on high
Mounts, from our mighty thoughts and from the
      fount
Of sense untellable, Beauty
That seems to be some quivering splendour cast
By the immortal nature on this quicksand,

And by surhuman fates
Given to mortal state
To be a sign and an hope made secure
Of blissful kingdoms and the aureate spheres;
And on the morrow, by some lightsome twist,
Shameful in sight, abject, abominable
All this angelic aspect can return
And be but what it was
With all the admirable concepts that moved from it
Swept from the mind with it in its departure.

Infinite things desired, lofty visions
'Got on desirous thought by natural virtue,
And the wise concord, whence through delicious seas
The arcane spirit of the whole Mankind
Turns hardy pilot . . . and if one wrong note
Strike the tympanum,
Instantly
That paradise is hurled to nothingness.

O mortal nature,
If thou art
Frail and so vile in all,
How canst thou reach so high with thy poor sense;
Yet if thou art
Noble in any part
How is the noblest of thy speech and thought
So lightly wrought
Or to such base occasion lit and quenched?

SATIEMUS

WHAT if I know thy speeches word by word?
    And if thou knew'st I knew them wouldst
        thou speak?
What if I know thy speeches word by word,
And all the time thou sayest them o'er I said,
"Lo, one there was who bent her fair bright head,
Sighing as thou dost through the golden speech."
Or, as our laughters mingle each with each,
As crushed lips take their respite fitfully,
What if my thoughts were turned in their mid reach
Whispering among them, "The fair dead
Must know such moments, thinking on the grass;
On how white dogwoods murmured overhead
In the bright glad days!"
How if the low dear sound within thy throat
Hath as faint lute-strings in its dim accord
Dim tales that blind me, running one by one
With times told over as we tell by rote;
What if I know thy laughter word by word
Nor find aught novel in thy merriment?

MR. HOUSMAN'S MESSAGE

O WOE, woe,
    People are born and die,
      We also shall be dead pretty soon
Therefore let us act as if we were
        dead already.

The bird sits on the hawthorn tree
But he dies also, presently.
Some lads get hung, and some get shot.
Woeful is this human lot.
      Woe! woe, etcetera. . . .

London is a woeful place,
Shropshire is much pleasanter.
Then let us smile a little space
Upon fond nature's morbid grace.
Oh, Woe, woe, woe, etcetera. . . .

TRANSLATIONS AND ADAPTATIONS FROM HEINE

FROM "DIE HEIMKEHR"

I

IS your hate, then, of such measure?
  Do you, truly, so detest me?
    Through all the world will I complain
Of *how* you have addressed me.

O ye lips that are ungrateful,
Hath it never once distressed you,
That you can say such *awful* things
Of *any* one who ever kissed you?

II

SO thou hast forgotten fully
  That I so long held thy heart wholly,
    Thy little heart, so sweet and false and small
That there's no thing more sweet or false at all.

Love and lay thou hast forgotten fully,
And my heart worked at them unduly.
I know not if the love or if the lay were better stuff,
But I know now, they both were good enough.

III

TELL me where thy lovely love is,
  Whom thou once did sing so sweetly,
  When the fairy flames enshrouded
Thee, and held thy heart completely.

All the flames are dead and sped now
And my heart is cold and sere;
Behold this book, the urn of ashes,
'Tis my true love's sepulchre.

IV

I DREAMT that I was God Himself
  Whom heavenly joy immerses,
  And all the angels sat about
And praised my verses.

V

THE mutilated choir boys
  When I begin to sing
  Complain about the awful noise
And call my voice too thick a thing.

When light their voices lift them up,
Bright notes against the ear,
Through trills and runs like crystal,
Ring delicate and clear.

They sing of Love that's grown desirous,
Of Love, and joy that is Love's inmost part,
And all the ladies swim through tears
Toward such a work of art.

THIS delightful young man
 Should not lack for honourers,
 He propitiates me with oysters,
With Rhine wine and liqueurs.

How his coat and pants adorn him!
Yet his ties are more adorning,
In these he daily comes to ask me:
"Are you feeling well this morning?"

He speaks of my extended fame,
My wit, charm, definitions,
And is diligent to serve me,
Is detailed in his provisions.

In evening company he sets his face
In most spirit*el* positions,
And declaims before the ladies
My *god-like* compositions.

O what comfort is it for me
To find him such, when the days bring
No comfort, at my time of life when
All good things go vanishing.

TRANSLATOR TO TRANSLATED

O Harry Heine, curses be,
I live too late to sup with thee!
Who can demolish at such polished ease
Philistia's pomp and Art's pomposities!

VII

I AM the Princess Ilza
In Ilsenstein I fare,
Come with me to that castle
And we'll be happy there.

Thy head will I cover over
With my waves' clarity
Till thou forget thy sorrow,
O wounded sorrowfully.

Thou wilt in my white arms there,
Nay, on my breast thou must
Forget and rest and dream there
For thine old legend-lust.

My lips and my heart are thine there
As they were his and mine.
His? Why the good King Harry's,
And he is dead lang syne.

Dead men stay alway dead men,
Life is the live man's part,
And I am fair and golden
With joy breathless at heart.

If my heart stay below there,
My crystal halls ring clear
To the dance of lords and ladies
In all their splendid gear.

The silken trains go rustling,
The spur-clinks sound between,
The dark dwarfs blow and bow there
Small horn and violin.

Yet shall my white arms hold thee,
That bound King Harry about.
Ah, I covered his ears with them
When the trumpet rang out.

VIII

NIGHT SONG

AND have you thoroughly kissed my lips?
There was no particular haste,
And are you not ready when evening's come?
There's no *particular* haste.

You've got the whole night before you,
Heart's-all-belovèd-my-own;
In an uninterrupted night one can
Get a good deal of kissing done.

THE HOUSE OF SPLENDOUR

'TIS Evanoe's,
   A house not made with hands,
      But out somewhere beyond the worldly ways
Her gold is spread, above, around, inwoven;
Strange ways and walls are fashioned out of it.

And I have seen my Lady in the sun,
Her hair was spread about, a sheaf of wings,
And red the sunlight was, behind it all.

And I have seen her there within her house,
With six great sapphires hung along the wall,
Low, panel-shaped, a-level with her knees,
And all her robe was woven of pale gold.

There are there many rooms and all of gold,
Of woven walls deep patterned, of email,
Of beaten work; and through the claret stone,
Set to some weaving, comes the aureate light.

Here am I come perforce my love of her,
Behold mine adoration
Maketh me clear, and there are powers in this
Which, played on by the virtues of her soul,
Break down the four-square walls of standing time.

THE FLAME

'TIS not a game that plays at mates and
      mating,
    Provençe knew;
'Tis not a game of barter, lands and houses,
Provençe knew.
We who are wise beyond your dream of wisdom,
Drink our immortal moments; we "pass through."
We have gone forth beyond your bonds and borders,
Provençe knew;
And all the tales of Oisin say but this:
That man doth pass the net of days and hours.
Where time is shrivelled down to time's seed corn
We of the Ever-living, in that light
Meet through our veils and whisper, and of love.

O smoke and shadow of a darkling world,
These, and the rest, and all the rest we knew.

'Tis not a game that plays at mates and mating,
'Tis not a game of barter, lands and houses,
'Tis not "of days and nights" and troubling years,
Of cheeks grown sunken and glad hair gone gray;
There *is* the subtler music, the clear light
Where time burns back about th' eternal embers.
We are not shut from all the thousand heavens:
Lo, there are many gods whom we have seen,
Folk of unearthly fashion, places splendid,
Bulwarks of beryl and of chrysoprase.

Sapphire Benacus, in thy mists and thee
Nature herself's turned metaphysical,
Who can look on that blue and not believe?

Thou hooded opal, thou eternal pearl,
O thou dark secret with a shimmering floor,
Through all thy various mood I know thee mine;

If I have merged my soul, or utterly
Am solved and bound in, through aught here on
    earth,
There canst thou find me, O thou anxious thou,
Who call'st about my gates for some lost me;
I say my soul flowed back, became translucent.
Search not my lips, O Love, let go my hands,
This thing that moves as man is no more mortal.
If thou hast seen my shade sans character,
If thou hast seen that mirror of all moments,
That glass to all things that o'ershadow it,
Call not that mirror me, for I have slipped
Your grasp, I have eluded.

HORAE BEATAE INSCRIPTIO

HOW will this beauty, when I am far hence,
    Sweep back upon me and engulf my mind!

How will these hours, when we twain are gray,
Turned in their sapphire tide, come flooding o'er us!

THE ALTAR

LET us build here an exquisite friendship,
    The flame, the autumn, and the green rose of
        love
Fought out their strife here, 'tis a place of wonder;
Where these have been, meet 'tis, the ground is holy.

AU SALON

Her grave, sweet haughtiness
Pleaseth me, and in like wise
Her quiet ironies.
Others are beautiful, none more, some less.

I SUPPOSE, when poetry comes down to facts,
When our souls are returned to the gods
                And the spheres they belong in,
Here in the every-day where our acts
Rise up and judge us;

I suppose there are a few dozen verities
That no shift of mood can shake from us:

One place where we'd rather have tea
(Thus far hath modernity brought us)
"Tea" (Damn you!)
                Have tea, damn the Caesars,
Talk of the latest success, give wing to some scandal,
Garble a name we detest, and for prejudice?
Set loose the whole consummate pack
                to bay like Sir Roger de Coverley's

This our reward for our works,
                sic crescit gloria mundi:
Some circle of not more than three
                that we prefer to play up to,
Some few whom we'd rather please
                than hear the whole aegrum vulgus
Splitting its beery jowl
                a-meaowling our praises.

Some certain peculiar things,
                cari laresque, penates,
Some certain accustomed forms,
                the absolute unimportant.

AU JARDIN

O YOU away high there,
     you that lean
  From amber lattices upon the cobalt night,
I am below amid the pine trees,
Amid the little pine trees, hear me!

"The jester walked in the garden."
       Did he so?
Well, there's no use your loving me
That way, Lady;
For I've nothing but songs to give you.

I am set wide upon the world's ways
To say that life is, some way, a gay thing,
But you never string two days upon one wire
But there'll come sorrow of it.
      And I loved a love once,
Over beyond the moon there,
     I loved a love once,
And, may be, more times,

But she danced like a pink moth in the shrubbery.

Oh, I know you women from the "other folk,"
And it'll all come right,
O' Sundays.

"The jester walked in the garden."
       Did he so?

RIPOSTES

1912

RIPOSTES

EZRA POUND

SILET

WHEN I behold how black, immortal ink
    Drips from my deathless pen—ah, well-
       away!
Why should we stop at all for what I think?
There is enough in what I chance to say.

It is enough that we once came together;
What is the use of setting it to rime?
When it is autumn do we get spring weather,
Or gather may of harsh northwindish time?

It is enough that we once came together;
What if the wind have turned against the rain?
It is enough that we once came together;
Time has seen this, and will not turn again;

And who are we, who know that last intent,
To plague to-morrow with a testament!

Verona 1911

IN EXITUM CUIUSDAM

On a certain one's departure

"TIME'S bitter flood"!   Oh, that's all very
    well,
    But where's the old friend hasn't fallen off,
Or slacked his hand-grip when you first gripped
   fame?
I know your circle and can fairly tell
What you have kept and what you've left behind:
I know my circle and know very well
How many faces I'd have out of mind.

THE TOMB AT AKR ÇAAR

"I AM thy soul, Nikoptis. I have watched
These five millenia, and thy dead eyes
Moved not, nor ever answer my desire,
And thy light limbs, wherethrough I leapt aflame,
Burn not with me nor any saffron thing.

See, the light grass sprang up to pillow thee,
And kissed thee with a myriad grassy tongues;
But not thou me.
I have read out the gold upon the wall,
And wearied out my thought upon the signs.
And there is no new thing in all this place.

I have been kind. See, I have left the jars sealed,
Lest thou shouldst wake and whimper for thy wine.
And all thy robes I have kept smooth on thee.

O thou unmindful! How should I forget!
—Even the river many days ago,
The river? thou wast over young.
And three souls came upon Thee—
And I came.
And I flowed in upon thee, beat them off;
I have been intimate with thee, known thy ways.
Have I not touched thy palms and finger-tips,
Flowed in, and through thee and about thy heels?
How 'came I in'? Was I not thee and Thee?

And no sun comes to rest me in this place,
And I am torn against the jagged dark,
And no light beats upon me, and you say
No word, day after day.

Oh! I could get me out, despite the marks
And all their crafty work upon the door,
Out through the glass-green fields. . . .
    .   .   .   .
Yet it is quiet here:
I do not go."

PORTRAIT D'UNE FEMME

YOUR mind and you are our Sargasso Sea,
London has swept about you this score years
And bright ships left you this or that in fee:
Ideas, old gossip, oddments of all things,
Strange spars of knowledge and dimmed wares of
    price.
Great minds have sought you—lacking someone else.
You have been second always. Tragical?
No. You preferred it to the usual thing:
One dull man, dulling and uxorious,
One average mind—with one thought less, each
    year.
Oh, you are patient, I have seen you sit
Hours, where something might have floated up.
And now you pay one. Yes, you richly pay.
You are a person of some interest, one comes to you
And takes strange gain away:
Trophies fished up; some curious suggestion;
Fact that leads nowhere; and a tale or two,
Pregnant with mandrakes, or with something else
That might prove useful and yet never proves,
That never fits a corner or shows use,
Or finds its hour upon the loom of days:
The tarnished, gaudy, wonderful old work;
Idols and ambergris and rare inlays,
These are your riches, your great store; and yet
For all this sea-hoard of deciduous things,
Strange woods half sodden, and new brighter stuff:
In the slow float of differing light and deep,
No! there is nothing! In the whole and all,
Nothing that's quite your own.
                Yet this is you.

N. Y.

MY City, my beloved, my white! Ah, slender,
Listen! Listen to me, and I will breathe
into thee a soul.
Delicately upon the reed, attend me!

Now do I know that I am mad,
For here are a million people surly with traffic;
This is no maid.
Neither could I play upon any reed if I had one.

My City, my beloved,
Thou art a maid with no breasts,
Thou art slender as a silver reed.
Listen to me, attend me!
And I will breathe into thee a soul,
And thou shalt live for ever.

A GIRL

THE tree has entered my hands,
The sap has ascended my arms,
The tree has grown in my breast—
Downward,
The branches grow out of me, like arms.

Tree you are,
Moss you are,
You are violets with wind above them.
A child—*so* high—you are,
And all this is folly to the world.

"PHASELLUS ILLE"

THIS *papier-mâché*, which you see, my friends,
    Saith 'twas the worthiest of editors.
    Its mind was made up in "the seventies,"
Nor hath it ever since changed that concoction.
It works to represent that school of thought
Which brought the hair-cloth chair to such perfec-
    tion,
Nor will the horrid threats of Bernard Shaw
Shake up the stagnant pool of its convictions;
Nay, should the deathless voice of all the world
Speak once again for its sole stimulation,
'Twould not move it one jot from left to right.

Come Beauty barefoot from the Cyclades,
She'd find a model for St. Anthony
In this thing's sure *decorum* and behaviour.

AN OBJECT

THIS thing, that hath a code and not a core,
    Hath set acquaintance where might be
        affections,
And nothing now
        Disturbeth his reflections.

QUIES

THIS is another of our ancient loves.
    Pass and be silent, Rullus, for the day
    Hath lacked a something since this lady
    passed;
Hath lacked a something. 'Twas but marginal.

THE SEAFARER

From the Anglo-Saxon

MAY I for my own self song's truth reckon,
Journey's jargon, how I in harsh days
Hardship endured oft.
Bitter breast-cares have I abided,
Known on my keel many a care's hold,
And dire sea-surge, and there I oft spent
Narrow nightwatch nigh the ship's head
While she tossed close to cliffs. Coldly afflicted,
My feet were by frost benumbed.
Chill its chains are; chafing sighs
Hew my heart round and hunger begot
Mere-weary mood. Lest man know not
That he on dry land loveliest liveth,
List how I, care-wretched, on ice-cold sea,
Weathered the winter, wretched outcast
Deprived of my kinsmen;
Hung with hard ice-flakes, where hail-scur flew,
There I heard naught save the harsh sea
And ice-cold wave, at whiles the swan cries,
Did for my games the gannet's clamour,
Sea-fowls' loudness was for me laughter,
The mews' singing all my mead-drink.
Storms, on the stone-cliffs beaten, fell on the stern
In icy feathers; full oft the eagle screamed
With spray on his pinion.
                    Not any protector
May make merry man faring needy.
This he little believes, who aye in winsome life
Abides 'mid burghers some heavy business,
Wealthy and wine-flushed, how I weary oft
Must bide above brine.
Neareth nightshade, snoweth from north,
Frost froze the land, hail fell on earth then,
Corn of the coldest. Nathless there knocketh now

The heart's thought that I on high streams
The salt-wavy tumult traverse alone.
Moaneth alway my mind's lust
That I fare forth, that I afar hence
Seek out a foreign fastness.
For this there's no mood-lofty man over earth's
    midst,
Not though he be given his good, but will have in
    his youth greed;
Nor his deed to the daring, nor his king to the
    faithful
But shall have his sorrow for sea-fare
Whatever his lord will.
He hath not heart for harping, nor in ring-having
Nor winsomeness to wife, nor world's delight
Nor any whit else save the wave's slash,
Yet longing comes upon him to fare forth on the water.
Bosque taketh blossom, cometh beauty of berries,
Fields to fairness, land fares brisker,
All this admonisheth man eager of mood,
The heart turns to travel so that he then thinks
On flood-ways to be far departing.
Cuckoo calleth with gloomy crying,
He singeth summerward, bodeth sorrow,
The bitter heart's blood. Burgher knows not—
He the prosperous man—what some perform
Where wandering them widest draweth.
So that but now my heart burst from my breastlock,
My mood 'mid the mere-flood,
Over the whale's acre, would wander wide.
On earth's shelter cometh oft to me,
Eager and ready, the crying lone-flyer,
Whets for the whale-path the heart irresistibly,
O'er tracks of ocean; seeing that anyhow
My lord deems to me this dead life
On loan and on land, I believe not

That any earth-weal eternal standeth
Save there be somewhat calamitous
That, ere a man's tide go, turn it to twain.
Disease or oldness or sword-hate
Beats out the breath from doom-gripped body.
And for this, every earl whatever, for those speak-
    ing after—
Laud of the living, boasteth some last word,
That he will work ere he pass onward,
Frame on the fair earth 'gainst foes his malice,
Daring ado, . . .
So that all men shall honour him after
And his laud beyond them remain 'mid the English,
Aye, for ever, a lasting life's-blast,
Delight 'mid the doughty.
                    Days little durable,
And all arrogance of earthen riches,
There come now no kings nor Cæsars
Nor gold-giving lords like those gone.
Howe'er in mirth most magnified,
Whoe'er lived in life most lordliest,
Drear all this excellence, delights undurable!
Waneth the watch, but the world holdeth.
Tomb hideth trouble. The blade is layed low.
Earthly glory ageth and seareth.
No man at all going the earth's gait,
But age fares against him, his face paleth,
Grey-haired he groaneth, knows gone companions,
Lordly men, are to earth o'ergiven,
Nor may he then the flesh-cover, whose life ceaseth,
Nor eat the sweet nor feel the sorry,
Nor stir hand nor think in mid heart,
And though he strew the grave with gold,
His born brothers, their buried bodies
Be an unlikely treasure hoard.

THE CLOAK [1]

THOU keep'st thy rose-leaf
   Till the rose-time will be over,
   Think'st thou that Death will kiss thee?
Think'st thou that the Dark House
   Will find thee such a lover
As I? Will the new roses miss thee?

Prefer my cloak unto the cloak of dust
   'Neath which the last year lies,
For thou shouldst more mistrust
   Time than my eyes.

[1] Asclepiades, Julianus Ægyptus.

Δώρια

BE in me as the eternal moods
      of the bleak wind, and not
   As transient things are—
      gaiety of flowers.
Have me in the strong loneliness
      of sunless cliffs
And of grey waters.
      Let the gods speak softly of us
In days hereafter,
      The shadowy flowers of Orcus
Remember thee.

67

APPARUIT

GOLDEN rose the house, in the portal I saw
thee, a marvel, carven in subtle stuff, a
portent.   Life died down in the lamp and flickered,
caught at the wonder.

Crimson, frosty with dew, the roses bend where
thou afar, moving in the glamorous sun,
drinkst in life of earth, of the air, the tissue
golden about thee.

Green the ways, the breath of the fields is thine there,
open lies the land, yet the steely going
darkly hast thou dared and the dreaded æther
parted before thee.

Swift at courage thou in the shell of gold, cast-
ing a-loose the cloak of the body, camest
straight, then shone thine oriel and the stunned light
faded about thee.

Half the graven shoulder, the throat aflash with
strands of light inwoven about it, loveli-
est of all things, frail alabaster, ah me!
swift in departing.

Clothed in goldish weft, delicately perfect,
gone as wind!   The cloth of the magical hands!
Thou a slight thing, thou in access of cunning
dar'dst to assume this?

THE NEEDLE

COME, or the stellar tide will slip away.
Eastward avoid the hour of its decline,
Now! for the needle trembles in my soul!

Here have we had our vantage, the good hour.
Here we have had our day, your day and mine.
Come now, before this power
That bears us up, shall turn against the pole.

Mock not the flood of stars, the thing's to be.
O Love, come now, this land turns evil slowly.
The waves bore in, soon will they bear away.

The treasure is ours, make we fast land with it.
Move we and take the tide, with its next favour,
Abide
Under some neutral force
Until this course turneth aside.

SUB MARE

IT is, and is not, I am sane enough,
Since you have come this place has hovered
round me,
This fabrication built of autumn roses,
Then there's a goldish colour, different.

And one gropes in these things as delicate
Algæ reach up and out, beneath
Pale slow green surgings of the underwave,
'Mid these things older than the names they have,
These things that are familiars of the god.

THE PLUNGE

I WOULD bathe myself in strangeness:
These comforts heaped upon me, smother me!
I burn, I scald so for the new,
New friends, new faces,
Places!
Oh to be out of this,
This that is all I wanted
      —save the new.

And you,
Love, you the much, the more desired!
Do I not loathe all walls, streets, stones,
All mire, mist, all fog,
All ways of traffic?
You, I would have flow over me like water,
Oh, but far out of this!
Grass, and low fields, and hills,
And sun,
Oh, sun enough!
Out, and alone, among some
Alien people!

A VIRGINAL

NO, no! Go from me. I have left her lately.
I will not spoil my sheath with lesser bright-
ness,
For my surrounding air hath a new lightness;
Slight are her arms, yet they have bound me straitly
And left me cloaked as with a gauze of æther;
As with sweet leaves; as with subtle clearness.
Oh, I have picked up magic in her nearness
To sheathe me half in half the things that sheathe
her.
No, no! Go from me. I have still the flavour,
Soft as spring wind that's come from birchen
bowers.
Green come the shoots, aye April in the branches,
As winter's wound with her sleight hand she
staunches,
Hath of the trees a likeness of the savour:
As white their bark, so white this lady's hours.

PAN IS DEAD

"**P**AN is dead. Great Pan is dead.
Ah! bow your heads, ye maidens all,
And weave ye him his coronal."

"There is no summer in the leaves,
And withered are the sedges;
How shall we weave a coronal,
Or gather floral pledges?"

"That I may not say, Ladies.
Death was ever a churl.
That I may not say, Ladies.
How should he show a reason,
That he has taken our Lord away
Upon such hollow season?"

DIEU! QU'IL LA FAIT

FROM CHARLES D'ORLEANS

GOD! that mad'st her well regard her,
How she is so fair and bonny;
For the great charms that are upon her
Ready are all folks to reward her.

Who could part him from her borders
When spells are alway renewed on her?
God! that mad'st her well regard her,
How she is so fair and bonny.

From here to there to the sea's border,
Dame nor damsel there's not any
Hath of perfect charms so many.
Thoughts of her are of dream's order:
God! that mad'st her well regard her.

THE PICTURE [1]

THE eyes of this dead lady speak to me,
    For here was love, was not to be drowned
        out.
And here desire, not to be kissed away.
The eyes of this dead lady speak to me.

[1] *Venus Reclining,* by Jacopo del Sellaio (1442-1493).

OF JACOPO DEL SELLAIO

THIS man knew out the secret ways of love,
    No man could paint such things who did not
        know.
And now she's gone, who was his Cyprian,
And you are here, who are "The Isles" to me.

And here's the thing that lasts the whole thing out:
The eyes of this dead lady speak to me.

THE RETURN

SEE, they return; ah, see the tentative
    Movements, and the slow feet,
    The trouble in the pace and the uncertain
Wavering!

See, they return, one, and by one,
With fear, as half-awakened;
As if the snow should hesitate
And murmur in the wind,
                and half turn back;
These were the "Wing'd-with-Awe,"
                Inviolable.

Gods of the wingèd shoe!
With them the silver hounds,
                sniffing the trace of air!

Haie! Haie!
        These were the swift to harry;
These the keen-scented;
These were the souls of blood.

Slow on the leash,
                pallid the leash-men!

THE ALCHEMIST

Chant for the Transmutation of Metals

SAÎL of Claustra, Aelis, Azalais,
   As you move among the bright trees;
   As your voices, under the larches of Paradise
Make a clear sound,
Saîl of Claustra, Aelis, Azalais,
Raimona, Tibors, Berangèrë,
'Neath the dark gleam of the sky;
Under night, the peacock-throated,
Bring the saffron-coloured shell,
Bring the red gold of the maple,
Bring the light of the birch tree in autumn
Mirals, Cembelins, Audiarda,
               Remember this fire.

Elain, Tireis, Alcmena
'Mid the silver rustling of wheat,
Agradiva, Anhes, Ardenca,
From the plum-coloured lake, in stillness,
From the molten dyes of the water
Bring the burnished nature of fire;
Briseis, Lianor, Loica,
From the wide earth and the olive,
From the poplars weeping their amber,
By the bright flame of the fishing torch
               Remember this fire.

Midonz, with the gold of the sun, the leaf of the
    poplar, by the light of the amber,
Midonz, daughter of the sun, shaft of the tree,
    silver of the leaf, light of the yellow of the
    amber,
Midonz, gift of the God, gift of the light, gift of
    the amber of the sun,
              Give light to the metal.
Anhes of Rocacoart, Ardenca, Aemelis,
From the power of grass,

From the white, alive in the seed,
From the heat of the bud,
From the copper of the leaf in autumn,
From the bronze of the maple, from the sap in the
    bough;
Lianor, Ioanna, Loica,
By the stir of the fin,
By the trout asleep in the gray-green of water;
Vanna, Mandetta, Viera, Alodetta, Picarda, Man-
    uela
From the red gleam of copper,
Ysaut, Ydone, slight rustling of leaves,
Vierna, Jocelynn, daring of spirits,
By the mirror of burnished copper,
                O Queen of Cypress,
Out of Erebus, the flat-lying breath,
Breath that is stretched out beneath the world:
Out of Erebus, out of the flat waste of air, lying
    beneath the world;
Out of the brown leaf-brown colourless
                Bring the imperceptible cool.
Elain, Tireis, Alcmena,
             Quiet this metal!
Let the manes put off their terror, let them put off
    their aqueous bodies with fire.
Let them assume the milk-white bodies of agate.
Let them draw together the bones of the metal.

Selvaggia, Guiscarda, Mandetta,
             Rain flakes of gold on the water
Azure and flaking silver of water,
Alcyon, Phætona, Alcmena,
Pallor of silver, pale lustre of Latona,
By these, from the malevolence of the dew
             Guard this alembic.
Elain, Tireis, Allodetta
        Quiet this metal.

LUSTRA

DEFINITION: LUSTRUM: an offering for the sins of
the whole people, made by the censors at the expira-
tion of their five years of office, etc. Elementary
Latin Dictionary of Charlton T. Lewis.

Vail de Lencour
Cui dono lepidum novum libellum.

And the days are not full enough
And the nights are not full enough
And life slips by like a field mouse
         Not shaking the grass.

TENZONE

WILL people accept them?
      (i.e. these songs).
    As a timorous wench from a centaur
      (or a centurion),
Already they flee, howling in terror.

Will they be touched with the verisimilitudes?
    Their virgin stupidity is untemptable.
I beg you, my friendly critics,
Do not set about to procure me an audience.

I mate with my free kind upon the crags;
    the hidden recesses
Have heard the echo of my heels,
      in the cool light,
      in the darkness.

THE CONDOLENCE

A mis soledades voy,
De mis soledades vengo,
Porque por andar conmigo
Mi bastan mis pensamientos.
Lope de Vega.

O MY fellow sufferers, songs of my youth,
A lot of asses praise you because you are
"virile,"
We, you, I! We are "Red Bloods"!
Imagine it, my fellow sufferers—
Our maleness lifts us out of the ruck,
Who'd have foreseen it?

O my fellow sufferers, we went out under the trees,
We were in especial bored with male stupidity.
We went forth gathering delicate thoughts,
Our *"fantastikon"* delighted to serve us.
We were not exasperated with women,
for the female is ductile.

And now you hear what is said to us:
We are compared to that sort of person
Who wanders about announcing his sex
As if he had just discovered it.
Let us leave this matter, my songs,
and return to that which concerns us.

THE GARRET

COME, let us pity those who are better off
                than we are.
        Come, my friend, and remember
                that the rich have butlers and no friends,
And we have friends and no butlers.
Come, let us pity the married and the unmarried.

Dawn enters with little feet
                like a gilded Pavlova,
And I am near my desire.
Nor has life in it aught better
Than this hour of clear coolness,
                the hour of waking together.

THE GARDEN

En robe de parade.
                                    Samain

LIKE a skein of loose silk blown against a wall
        She walks by the railing of a path in Ken-
                sington Gardens,
And she is dying piece-meal
                of a sort of emotional anæmia.

And round about there is a rabble
Of the filthy, sturdy, unkillable infants of the very
                poor.
They shall inherit the earth.

In her is the end of breeding.
Her boredom is exquisite and excessive.
She would like some one to speak to her,
And is almost afraid that I
                will commit that indiscretion.

ORTUS

HOW have I laboured?
　　How have I not laboured
　　To bring her soul to birth,
To give these elements a name and a centre!
She is beautiful as the sunlight, and as fluid.
She has no name, and no place.
How have I laboured to bring her soul into
　　separation;
To give her a name and her being!

Surely you are bound and entwined,
You are mingled with the elements unborn;
I have loved a stream and a shadow.

I beseech you enter your life.
I beseech you learn to say "I,"
When I question you;
For you are no part, but a whole,
No portion, but a being.

SALUTATION

O GENERATION of the thoroughly smug
      and thoroughly uncomfortable,
   I have seen fishermen picnicking in the sun,
I have seen them with untidy families,
I have seen their smiles full of teeth
      and heard ungainly laughter.
And I am happier than you are,
And they were happier than I am;
And the fish swim in the lake
      and do not even own clothing.

SALUTATION THE SECOND

YOU were praised, my books,
         because I had just come from the country;
   I was twenty years behind the times
      so you found an audience ready.
I do not disown you,
      do not you disown your progeny.

Here they stand without quaint devices,
Here they are with nothing archaic about them.
Observe the irritation in general:

"Is this," they say, "the nonsense
         that we expect of poets?"
"Where is the Picturesque?"
         "Where is the vertigo of emotion?"
"No! his first work was the best."
         "Poor Dear! he has lost his illusions."

Go, little naked and impudent songs,
Go with a light foot!

(Or with two light feet, if it please you!)
Go and dance shamelessly!
Go with an impertinent frolic!

Greet the grave and the stodgy,
Salute them with your thumbs at your noses.

Here are your bells and confetti.
Go! rejuvenate things!
Rejuvenate even "The Spectator."
      Go! and make cat calls!
Dance and make people blush,
Dance the dance of the phallus
      and tell anecdotes of Cybele!
Speak of the indecorous conduct of the Gods!
      (Tell it to Mr. Strachey)

Ruffle the skirts of prudes,
      speak of their knees and ankles.
But, above all, go to practical people—
      go! jangle their door-bells!
Say that you do no work
      and that you will live forever.

THE SPRING

Ἦρι μὲν αἵ τε κυδώνιαι—IBYCUS.

CYDONIAN Spring with her attendant train,
  Maelids and water-girls,
    Stepping beneath a boisterous wind from
    Thrace,
Throughout this sylvan place
Spreads the bright tips,
And every vine-stock is
Clad in new brilliancies.
                    And wild desire
Falls like black lightning.
O bewildered heart,
Though every branch have back what last year lost,
She, who moved here amid the cyclamen,
Moves only now a clinging tenuous ghost.

ALBATRE

THIS lady in the white bath-robe which she
  calls a peignoir,
    Is, for the time being, the mistress of my
    friend,
And the delicate white feet of her little white dog
Are not more delicate than she is,
Nor would Gautier himself have despised their con-
            trasts in whiteness
As she sits in the great chair
Between the two indolent candles.

CAUSA

I JOIN these words for four people,
Some others may overhear them,
O world, I am sorry for you,
You do not know these four people.

COMMISSION

GO, my songs, to the lonely and the unsatisfied,
Go also to the nerve-wracked, go to the en-
slaved-by-convention,
Bear to them my contempt for their oppressors.
Go as a great wave of cool water,
Bear my contempt of oppressors.

Speak against unconscious oppression,
Speak against the tyranny of the unimaginative,
Speak against bonds.
Go to the bourgeoise who is dying of her ennuis,
Go to the women in suburbs.
Go to the hideously wedded,
Go to them whose failure is concealed,
Go to the unluckily mated,
Go to the bought wife,
Go to the woman entailed.

Go to those who have delicate lust,
Go to those whose delicate desires are thwarted,
Go like a blight upon the dulness of the world;
Go with your edge against this,
Strengthen the subtle cords,
Bring confidence upon the algæ and the tentacles of
the soul.

Go in a friendly manner,
Go with an open speech.
Be eager to find new evils and new good,
Be against all forms of oppression.
Go to those who are thickened with middle age,
To those who have lost their interest.

Go to the adolescent who are smothered in family—
Oh how hideous it is
To see three generations of one house gathered
    together!
It is like an old tree with shoots,
And with some branches rotted and falling.

Go out and defy opinion,
Go against this vegetable bondage of the blood.
Be against all sorts of mortmain.

A PACT

I MAKE a pact with you, Walt Whitman—
I have detested you long enough.
    I come to you as a grown child
Who has had a pig-headed father;
I am old enough now to make friends.
It was you that broke the new wood,
Now is a time for carving.
We have one sap and one root—
Let there be commerce between us.

SURGIT FAMA

THERE is a truce among the gods,
Korè is seen in the North
Skirting the blue-gray sea
In gilded and russet mantle.
The corn has again its mother and she, Leuconoë,
That failed never women,
Fails not the earth now.

The tricksome Hermes is here;
He moves behind me
Eager to catch my words,
Eager to spread them with rumour;
To set upon them his change
Crafty and subtle;
To alter them to his purpose;
But do thou speak true, even to the letter:

"Once more in Delos, once more is the altar a-quiver.
Once more is the chant heard.
Once more are the never abandoned gardens
Full of gossip and old tales."

DANCE FIGURE

For the Marriage in Cana of Galilee

DARK eyed,
 O woman of my dreams,
 Ivory sandaled,
There is none like thee among the dancers,
None with swift feet.

I have not found thee in the tents,
In the broken darkness.
I have not found thee at the well-head
Among the women with pitchers.

Thine arms are as a young sapling under the bark;
Thy face as a river with lights.

White as an almond are thy shoulders;
As new almonds stripped from the husk.
They guard thee not with eunuchs;
Not with bars of copper.

Gilt turquoise and silver are in the place of thy rest.
A brown robe, with threads of gold woven in pat-
    terns, hast thou gathered about thee,
O Nathat-Ikanaie, "Tree-at-the-river."

As a rillet among the sedge are thy hands upon me;
Thy fingers a frosted stream.

Thy maidens are white like pebbles;
Their music about thee!

There is none like thee among the dancers;
None with swift feet.

APRIL

Nympharum membra disjecta

THREE spirits came to me
And drew me apart
To where the olive boughs
Lay stripped upon the ground:
Pale carnage beneath bright mist.

GENTILDONNA

SHE passed and left no quiver in the veins, who
now
Moving among the trees, and clinging
in the air she severed,
Fanning the grass she walked on then, endures:

Grey olive leaves beneath a rain-cold sky.

THE REST

O HELPLESS few in my country,
O remnant enslaved!

Artists broken against her,
A-stray, lost in the villages,
Mistrusted, spoken-against,

Lovers of beauty, starved,
Thwarted with systems,
Helpless against the control;

You who can not wear yourselves out
By persisting to successes,
You who can only speak,
Who can not steel yourselves into reiteration;

You of the finer sense,
Broken against false knowledge,
You who can know at first hand,
Hated, shut in, mistrusted:

Take thought:
I have weathered the storm,
I have beaten out my exile.

LES MILLWIN

THE little Millwins attend the Russian Ballet.
The mauve and greenish souls of the little
Millwins
Were seen lying along the upper seats
Like so many unused boas.

The turbulent and undisciplined host of art
students—
The rigorous deputation from "Slade"—
Was before them.

With arms exalted, with fore-arms
Crossed in great futuristic X's, the art students
Exulted, they beheld the splendours of *Cleopatra*.

And the little Millwins beheld these things;
With their large and anæmic eyes they looked out
upon this configuration.

Let us therefore mention the fact,
For it seems to us worthy of record.

FURTHER INSTRUCTIONS

COME, my songs, let us express our baser pas-
            sions,
    Let us express our envy of the man with a
    steady job and no worry about the future.
You are very idle, my songs.
I fear you will come to a bad end.
You stand about in the streets,
You loiter at the corners and bus-stops,
You do next to nothing at all.

You do not even express our inner nobilities,
You will come to a very bad end.

And I?
I have gone half cracked,
I have talked to you so much that
                        I almost see you about me,
Insolent little beasts, shameless, devoid of clothing!

But you, newest song of the lot,
You are not old enough to have done much mischief,
I will get you a green coat out of China
With dragons worked upon it,
I will get you the scarlet silk trousers
From the statue of the infant Christ in Santa Maria
        Novella,
Lest they say we are lacking in taste,
Or that there is no caste in this family.

A SONG OF THE DEGREES

I

REST me with Chinese colours,
For I think the glass is evil.

II

The wind moves above the wheat—
With a silver crashing,
A thin war of metal.

I have known the golden disc,
I have seen it melting above me.
I have known the stone-bright place,
The hall of clear colours.

III

O glass subtly evil, O confusion of colours!
O light bound and bent in, O soul of the captive,
Why am I warned?   Why am I sent away?
Why is your glitter full of curious mistrust?
O glass subtle and cunning, O powdery gold!
O filaments of amber, two-faced iridescence!

ITÉ

GO, my songs, seek your praise from the young
and from the intolerant,
Move among the lovers of perfection alone.
Seek ever to stand in the hard Sophoclean light
And take your wounds from it gladly.

DUM CAPITOLIUM SCANDET

HOW many will come after me
      singing as well as I sing, none better;
   Telling the heart of their truth
   as I have taught them to tell it;
Fruit of my seed,
   O my unnameable children.
Know then that I loved you from afore-time,
Clear speakers, naked in the sun, untrammelled.

Τὸ Καλόν

Even in my dreams you have denied yourself to
   me
And sent me only your handmaids.

THE STUDY IN AESTHETICS

THE very small children in patched clothing,
   Being smitten with an unusual wisdom,
   Stopped in their play as she passed them
And cried up from their cobbles:

   Guarda! Ahi, guarda! ch' è be'a![1]

But three years after this
I heard the young Dante, whose last name I do not
   know—
For there are, in Sirmione, twenty-eight young
   Dantes and thirty-four Catulli;
And there had been a great catch of sardines,
And his elders
Were packing them in the great wooden boxes

[1] *Bella.*

96

For the market in Brescia, and he
Leapt about, snatching at the bright fish
And getting in both of their ways;
And in vain they commanded him to *sta fermo!*
And when they would not let him arrange
The fish in the boxes
He stroked those which were already arranged,
Murmuring for his own satisfaction
This identical phrase:

    Ch' è be'a.

And at this I was mildly abashed.

THE BELLAIRES

Aus meinen grossen Schmerzen
Mach' ich die kleinen Lieder

THE good Bellaires
    Do not understand the conduct of this
    world's affairs.
In fact they understood them so badly
That they have had to cross the Channel.
Nine lawyers, four counsels, five judges and three
    proctors of the King,
Together with the respective wives, husbands, sis-
    ters and heterogeneous connections of the good
    Bellaires,
Met to discuss their affairs;
But the good Bellaires have so little understood
    their affairs
That now there is no one at all
Who can understand any affair of theirs. Yet
Fourteen hunters still eat in the stables of
The good Squire Bellaire;

But these may not suffer attainder,
For they may not belong to the good Squire Bel-
    laire
But to his wife.
On the contrary, if they do not belong to his wife,
He will plead
A "freedom from attainder"
For twelve horses and also for twelve boarhounds
From Charles the Fourth;
And a further freedom for the remainder
Of horses, from Henry the Fourth.
But the judges,
Being free of mediæval scholarship,
Will pay no attention to this,
And there will be only the more confusion,
Replevin, estoppel, espavin and what not.

Nine lawyers, four counsels, etc.,
Met to discuss their affairs,
But the sole result was bills
From lawyers to whom no one was indebted,
And even the lawyers
Were uncertain who was supposed to be indebted
    to them.

Wherefore the good Squire Bellaire
Resides now at Agde and Biaucaire.
To Carcassonne, Pui, and Alais
He fareth from day to day,
Or takes the sea air
Between Marseilles
And Beziers.
And for all this I have considerable regret,
For the good Bellaires
Are very charming people.

THE NEW CAKE OF SOAP

LO, how it gleams and glistens in the sun
Like the cheek of a Chesterton.

SALVATIONISTS

I

COME, my songs, let us speak of perfection—
We shall get ourselves rather disliked.

II

Ah yes, my songs, let us resurrect
The very excellent term *Rusticus.*
Let us apply it in all its opprobrium
To those to whom it applies.
And you may decline to make them immortal,
For we shall consider them and their state
In delicate
Opulent silence.

III

Come, my songs,
Let us take arms against this sea of stupidities—
Beginning with Mumpodorus;
And against this sea of vulgarities—
Beginning with Nimmim;
And against this sea of imbeciles—
All the Bulmenian literati.

EPITAPH

LEUCIS, who intended a Grand Passion,
Ends with a willingness-to-oblige.

ARIDES

THE bashful Arides
    Has married an ugly wife,
    He was bored with his manner of life,
Indifferent and discouraged he thought he might as
Well do this as anything else.

Saying within his heart, "I am no use to myself,
"Let her, if she wants me, take me."
He went to his doom.

THE BATH TUB

AS a bathtub lined with white porcelain,
    When the hot water gives out or goes tepid,
    So is the slow cooling of our chivalrous pas-
        sion,
O my much praised but-not-altogether-satisfactory
    lady.

THE TEMPERAMENTS

NINE adulteries, 12 liaisons, 64 fornications
    and something approaching a rape
    Rest nightly upon the soul of our delicate
    friend Florialis,
And yet the man is so quiet and reserved in de-
    meanour
That he passes for both bloodless and sexless.
Bastidides, on the contrary, who both talks and
        writes of nothing save copulation,
Has become the father of twins,
But he accomplished this feat at some cost;
He had to be four times cuckold.

AMITIES

Old friends the most.—W. B. Y.

I

To one, on returning certain years after.

YOU wore the same quite correct clothing,
    You took no pleasure at all in my triumphs,
    You had the same old air of condescension
Mingled with a curious fear
    That I, myself, might have enjoyed them.
Te Voilà, mon Bourrienne, you also shall be immortal.

II

To another.

And we say good-bye to you also,
For you seem never to have discovered
That your relationship is wholly parasitic;
Yet to our feasts you bring neither
Wit, nor good spirits, nor the pleasing attitudes
    Of discipleship.

III

But you, *bos amic,* we keep on,
For to you we owe a real debt:
In spite of your obvious flaws,
You once discovered a moderate chop-house.

IV

    Iste fuit vir incultus,
    Deo laus, quod est sepultus,
    Vermes habent eius vultum
                  A-a-a-a—A-men.

    Ego autem jovialis
    Gaudero contubernalis
    Cum jocunda femina.

MEDITATIO

WHEN I carefully consider the curious habits
of dogs
I am compelled to conclude
That man is the superior animal.

When I consider the curious habits of man
I confess, my friend, I am puzzled.

TO DIVES

WHO am I to condemn you, O Dives,
I who am as much embittered
with poverty
As you are with useless riches?

LADIES

Agathas

FOUR and forty lovers had Agathas in the old
days,
All of whom she refused;
And now she turns to me seeking love,
And her hair also is turning.

Young Lady

I have fed your lar with poppies,
I have adored you for three full years;
And now you grumble because your dress does not fit
And because I happen to say so.

Lesbia Illa

Memnon, Memnon, that lady
Who used to walk about amongst us

With such gracious uncertainty,
Is now wedded
To a British householder.
Lugete, Veneres! Lugete, Cupidinesque!

PASSING

Flawless as Aphrodite,
Thoroughly beautiful,
Brainless,
The faint odour of your patchouli,
Faint, almost, as the lines of cruelty about your chin,
Assails me, and concerns me almost as little.

PHYLLIDULA

PHYLLIDULA is scrawny but amorous,
Thus have the gods awarded her,
That in pleasure she receives more than she
can give;
If she does not count this blessed
Let her change her religion.

THE PATTERNS

ERINNA is a model parent,
Her children have never discovered her
adulteries.
Lalage is also a model parent,
Her offspring are fat and happy.

CODA

O MY songs,
Why do you look so eagerly and so curiously
into people's faces,
Will you find your lost dead among them?

THE SEEING EYE

THE small dogs look at the big dogs;
     They observe unwieldly dimensions
     And curious imperfections of odor.
Here is a formal male group:
The young men look upon their seniors,
They consider the elderly mind
And observe its inexplicable correlations.

Said Tsin-Tsu:
It is only in small dogs and the young
That we find minute observation.

ANCORA

GOOD God! They say you are *risqué*,
     O canzonetti!
          We who went out into the four A. M. of the
               world
Composing our albas,
We who shook off our dew with the rabbits,
We who have seen even Artemis a-binding her
     sandals,
Have we ever heard the like?
O mountains of Hellas!!
Gather about me, O Muses!
When we sat upon the granite brink in Helicon
Clothed in the tattered sunlight,
O Muses with delicate shins,
O Muses with delectable knee-joints,
When we splashed and were splashed with
The lucid Castalian spray,
Had we ever such an epithet cast upon us!!

"DOMPNA POIS DE ME NO'US CAL"

FROM THE PROVENÇAL OF EN BERTRANS DE BORN

LADY, since you care nothing for me,
    And since you have shut me away from you
    Causelessly,
I know not where to go seeking,
For certainly
I will never again gather
Joy so rich, and if I find not ever
A lady with look so speaking
To my desire, worth yours whom I have lost,
I'll have no other love at any cost.

And since I could not find a peer to you,
Neither one so fair, nor of such heart,
So eager and alert,
Nor with such art
In attire, nor so gay
Nor with gift so bountiful and so true,
I will go out a-searching,
Culling from each a fair trait
To make me a borrowed lady
Till I again find you ready.

Bels Cembelins, I take of you your colour,
For it's your own, and your glance
Where love is,
A proud thing I do here,
For, as to colour and eyes
I shall have missed nothing at all,
Having yours.
I ask of Midons Aelis (of Montfort)
Her straight speech free-running,
That my phantom lack not in cunning.

At Chalais of the Viscountess, I would
That she give me outright
Her two hands and her throat,
So take I my road
To Rochechouart,
Swift-foot to my Lady Anhes,
Seeing that Tristan's lady Iseutz had never
Such grace of locks, I do ye to wit,
Though she'd the far fame for it.

Of Audiart at Malemort,
Though she with a full heart
Wish me ill,
I'd have her form that's laced
So cunningly,
Without blemish, for her love
Breaks not nor turns aside.
I of Miels-de-ben demand
Her straight fresh body,
She is so supple and young,
Her robes can but do her wrong.

Her white teeth, of the Lady Faidita
I ask, and the fine courtesy
She hath to welcome one,
And such replies she lavishes
Within her nest;
Of Bels Mirals, the rest,
Tall stature and gaiety,
To make these avail
She knoweth well, betide
No change nor turning aside.

Ah, Bels Senher, Maent, at last
I ask naught from you,
Save that I have such hunger for
This phantom

As I've for you, such flame-lap,
And yet I'd rather
Ask of you than hold another,
Mayhap, right close and kissed.
Ah, lady, why have you cast
Me out, knowing you hold me so fast!

THE COMING OF WAR: ACTAEON

AN image of Lethe,
  and the fields
   Full of faint light
    but golden,
Gray cliffs,
   and beneath them
A sea
Harsher than granite,
   unstill, never ceasing;
High forms
   with the movement of gods,
Perilous aspect;
   And one said:
"This is Actaeon."
   Actaeon of golden greaves!
Over fair meadows,
Over the cool face of that field,
Unstill, ever moving
Hosts of an ancient people,
The silent cortège.

AFTER CH'U YUAN

I WILL get me to the wood
Where the gods walk garlanded in wistaria,
By the silver blue flood
move others with ivory cars.
There come forth many maidens
to gather grapes for the leopards, my friend,
For there are leopards drawing the cars.

I will walk in the glade,
I will come out from the new thicket
and accost the procession of maidens.

By Wu'-ti

LIU CH'E

THE rustling of the silk is discontinued,
Dust drifts over the court-yard,
There is no sound of foot-fall, and the leaves
Scurry into heaps and lie still,
And she the rejoicer of the heart is beneath them :

A wet leaf that clings to the threshold.

FAN-PIECE, FOR HER IMPERIAL LORD

O FAN of white silk,
clear as frost on the grass-blade,
You also are laid aside.

TS'AI CHI'H

THE petals fall in the fountain,
the orange-coloured rose-leaves,
Their ochre clings to the stone.

IN A STATION OF THE METRO

THE apparition of these faces in the crowd;
Petals on a wet, black bough.

ALBA

AS cool as the pale wet leaves
                    of lily-of-the-valley
She lay beside me in the dawn.

HEATHER

THE black panther treads at my side,
And above my fingers
There float the petal-like flames.

The milk-white girls
Unbend from the holly-trees,
And their snow-white leopard
Watches to follow our trace.

THE FAUN

HA! sir, I have seen you sniffing and snoozling
                    about among my flowers.
And what, pray, do you know about
                    horticulture, you capriped?
"Come, Auster, come Apeliota,
And see the faun in our garden.
But if you move or speak
This thing will run at you
And scare itself to spasms."

COITUS

THE gilded phaloi of the crocuses
        are thrusting at the spring air.
    Here is there naught of dead gods
But a procession of festival,
A procession, O Giulio Romano,
Fit for your spirit to dwell in.
Dione, your nights are upon us.

The dew is upon the leaf.
The night about us is restless.

THE ENCOUNTER

ALL the while they were talking the new
        morality
    Her eyes explored me.
And when I arose to go
Her fingers were like the tissue
Of a Japanese paper napkin.

TEMPORA

IO! Io! Tamuz!
    The Dryad stands in my court-yard
    With plaintive, querulous crying.
(Tamuz. Io! Tamuz!)
Oh, no, she is not crying: "Tamuz."
She says, "May my poems be printed this week?
The god Pan is afraid to ask you,
May my poems be printed this week?"

BLACK SLIPPERS: BELLOTTI

AT the table beyond us
　　With her little suède slippers off,
　　With her white-stocking'd feet
Carefully kept from the floor by a napkin,
She converses:

　　　　"Connaissez-vous Ostende?"

The gurgling Italian lady on the other side of the
　　restaurant
Replies with a certain hauteur,
But I await with patience,
To see how Celestine will re-enter her slippers.
She re-enters them with a groan.

SOCIETY

THE family position was waning,
　　And on this account the little Aurelia,
　　Who had laughed on eighteen summers,
Now bears the palsied contact of Phidippus.

IMAGE FROM D'ORLEANS

YOUNG men riding in the street
　　In the bright new season
　　Spur without reason,
Causing their steeds to leap.

And at the pace they keep
Their horses' armoured feet
Strike sparks from the cobbled street
In the bright new season.

PAPYRUS

SPRING . . . .
Too long . . . . . .
Gongula . . . . . .

"IONE, DEAD THE LONG YEAR"

EMPTY are the ways,
Empty are the ways of this land
And the flowers
                    Bend over with heavy heads.
They bend in vain.
Empty are the ways of this land
                              Where Ione
Walked once, and now does not walk
But seems like a person just gone.

Ἰμέρρω

THY soul
Grown delicate with satieties,
Atthis.
O Atthis,
I long for thy lips.
I long for thy narrow breasts,
Thou restless, ungathered.

SHOP GIRL

FOR a moment she rested against me
Like a swallow half blown to the wall,
And they talk of Swinburne's women,
And the shepherdess meeting with Guido.
And the harlots of Baudelaire.

TO FORMIANUS' YOUNG LADY
FRIEND

After Valerius Catullus

ALL Hail! young lady with a nose
by no means too small,
With a foot unbeautiful,
and with eyes that are not black,
With fingers that are not long, and with a mouth
undry,
And with a tongue by no means too elegant,
You are the friend of Formianus, the vendor of
cosmetics,
And they call you beautiful in the province,
And you are even compared to Lesbia.

O most unfortunate age!

TAME CAT

"IT rests me to be among beautiful women.
Why should one always lie about such
matters?
I repeat:
It rests me to converse with beautiful women
Even though we talk nothing but nonsense,

The purring of the invisible antennæ
Is both stimulating and delightful."

L'ART, 1910

GREEN arsenic smeared on an egg-white cloth,
Crushed strawberries! Come, let us feast
our eyes.

SIMULACRA

WHY does the horse-faced lady of just the
unmentionable age
Walk down Longacre reciting Swinburne to
herself, inaudibly?
Why does the small child in the soiled-white imita-
tion fur coat
Crawl in the very black gutter beneath the grape
stand?
Why does the really handsome young woman ap-
proach me in Sackville Street
Undeterred by the manifest age of my trappings?

WOMEN BEFORE A SHOP

THE gew-gaws of false amber and false
turquoise attract them.
"Like to like nature": these agglutinous
yellows!

EPILOGUE

O CHANSONS foregoing
You were a seven days' wonder.
When you came out in the magazines
You created considerable stir in Chicago,
And now you are stale and worn out,
You're a very depleted fashion,
A hoop-skirt, a calash,
An homely, transient antiquity.
Only emotion remains.
Your emotions?
Are those of a maître-de-café.

THE SOCIAL ORDER

I

THIS government official
Whose wife is several years his senior,
Has such a caressing air
When he shakes hands with young ladies.

II

(Pompes Funèbres)

This old lady,
Who was "so old that she was an atheist,"
Is now surrounded
By six candles and a crucifix,
While the second wife of a nephew
Makes hay with the things in her house.
Her two cats
Go before her into Avernus;
A sort of chloroformed suttee,
And it is to be hoped that their spirits will walk
With their tails up,
And with a plaintive, gentle mewing,
For it is certain that she has left on this earth
No sound
Save a squabble of female connections.

THE TEA SHOP

THE girl in the tea shop
                    Is not so beautiful as she was,
        The August has worn against her.
She does not get up the stairs so eagerly;
Yes, she also will turn middle-aged,
And the glow of youth that she spread about us
                    As she brought us our muffins
Will be spread about us no longer.
                    She also will turn middle-aged.

ANCIENT MUSIC

WINTER is icummen in,
        Lhude sing Goddamm,
        Raineth drop and staineth slop,
And how the wind doth ramm!
                    Sing: Goddamm.
Skiddeth bus and sloppeth us,
An ague hath my ham.
Freezeth river, turneth liver,
                    Damn you, sing: Goddamm.
Goddamm, Goddamm, 'tis why I am, Goddamm,
                    So 'gainst the winter's balm.
Sing goddamm, damm, sing Goddamm,
Sing goddamm, sing goddamm, DAMM.

NOTE.—This is not folk music, but Dr. Ker writes that the tune
is to be found under the Latin words of a very ancient canon.

THE LAKE ISLE

O God, O Venus, O Mercury, patron of
   thieves,
      Give me in due time, I beseech you, a little
         tobacco-shop,
With the little bright boxes
      piled up neatly upon the shelves
And the loose fragrant cavendish
      and the shag,
And the bright Virginia
      loose under the bright glass cases,
And a pair of scales not too greasy,
And the whores dropping in for a word or two in
         passing,
For a flip word, and to tidy their hair a bit.

O God, O Venus, O Mercury, patron of thieves,
Lend me a little tobacco-shop,
      or install me in any profession
Save this damn'd profession of writing,
      where one needs one's brains all the time.

EPITAPHS

Fu I

FU I loved the high cloud and the hill,
   Alas, he died of alcohol.

Li Po

And Li Po also died drunk.
He tried to embrace a moon
In the Yellow River.

OUR CONTEMPORARIES

WHEN the Taihaitian princess
Heard that he had decided,
She rushed out into the sunlight and
swarmed up a cocoanut palm tree,

But he returned to this island
And wrote ninety Petrarchan sonnets.

NOTE.—Il s'agit d'un jeune poète qui a suivi le culte de Gauguin
jusqu'à Tahiti même (et qui vit encore). Etant fort bel homme,
quand la princesse bistre entendit qu'il voulait lui accorder ses
faveurs elle montra son allegresse de la façon dont nous venons de
parler. Malheureusement ses poèmes ne sont remplis que de ses
propres subjectivités, style Victorien de la "Georgian Anthology."

ANCIENT WISDOM, RATHER COSMIC

CHUANG-TZU dreamed,
And having dreamed that he was a bird, a
bee, and a butterfly,
He was uncertain why he should try to feel like any-
thing else,

Hence his contentment.

THE THREE POETS

CANDIDIA has taken a new lover
And three poets are gone into mourning.
The first has written a long elegy to
"Chloris,"
To "Chloris chaste and cold," his "only Chloris."
The second has written a sonnet
upon the mutability of woman,
And the third writes an epigram to Candidia.

THE GYPSY

"Est-ce que vous avez vu des autres—des camarades—avec des singes ou des ours?"

A Stray Gipsy—A.D. 1912

THAT was the top of the walk, when he said:
    "Have you seen any others, any of our lot,
    "With apes or bears?"
        —A brown upstanding fellow
Not like the half-castes,
        up on the wet road near Clermont.
The wind came, and the rain,
And mist clotted about the trees in the valley,
And I'd the long ways behind me,
        gray Arles and Biaucaire,
And he said, "Have you seen any of our lot?"
I'd seen a lot of his lot . . .
        ever since Rhodez,
Coming down from the fair
        of St. John,
With caravans, but never an ape or a bear.

THE GAME OF CHESS

DOGMATIC STATEMENT CONCERNING THE GAME OF CHESS:
THEME FOR A SERIES OF PICTURES

RED knights, brown bishops, bright queens,
   Striking the board, falling in strong "L"s of
      colour.
Reaching and striking in angles,
               holding lines in one colour.
This board is alive with light;
               these pieces are living in form,
Their moves break and reform the pattern:
               luminous green from the rooks,
Clashing with "X"s of queens,
               looped with the knight-leaps.

"Y" pawns, cleaving, embanking!
Whirl! Centripetal! Mate! King down in the
      vortex,
Clash, leaping of bands, straight strips of hard
      colour,
Blocked lights working in. Escapes. Renewal of
      contest.

PROVINCIA DESERTA

AT Rochecoart,
  Where the hills part
    in three ways,
And three valleys, full of winding roads,
Fork out to south and north,
There is a place of trees . . . gray with lichen.
I have walked there
    thinking of old days.
At Chalais
    is a pleached arbour;
Old pensioners and old protected women
Have the right there—
    it is charity.
I have crept over old rafters,
    peering down
Over the Dronne,
    over a stream full of lilies.
Eastward the road lies,
    Aubeterre is eastward,
With a garrulous old man at the inn.
I know the roads in that place:
Mareuil to the north-east,
    La Tour,
There are three keeps near Mareuil,
And an old woman,
    glad to hear Arnaut,
Glad to lend one dry clothing.

I have walked
    into Perigord,
I have seen the torch-flames, high-leaping,
Painting the front of that church;
Heard, under the dark, whirling laughter.
I have looked back over the stream
    and seen the high building,

Seen the long minarets, the white shafts.
I have gone in Riberac
                    and in Sarlat,
I have climbed rickety stairs, heard talk of Croy,
Walked over En Bertran's old layout,
Have seen Narbonne, and Cahors and Chalus,
Have seen Excideuil, carefully fashioned.

I have said:
                    "Here such a one walked.
"Here Cœur-de-Lion was slain.
                    "Here was good singing.
"Here one man hastened his step.
                    "Here one lay panting."
I have looked south from Hautefort,
                    thinking of Montaignac, southward.
I have lain in Rocafixada,
                    level with sunset,
Have seen the copper come down
                    tingeing the mountains,
I have seen the fields, pale, clear as an emerald,
Sharp peaks, high spurs, distant castles.
I have said: "The old roads have lain here.
"Men have gone by such and such valleys
"Where the great halls were closer together."
I have seen Foix on its rock, seen Toulouse, and
                    Arles greatly altered,
I have seen the ruined "Dorata."
                    I have said:
"Riquier! Guido."
                    I have thought of the second Troy,
Some little prized place in Auvergnat:
Two men tossing a coin, one keeping a castle,
One set on the highway to sing.
                    He sang a woman.
Auvergne rose to the song;
                    The Dauphin backed him.

"The castle to Austors!"
           "Pieire kept the singing—
"A fair man and a pleasant."
           He won the lady,
Stole her away for himself, kept her against armed
               force:
So ends that story.
That age is gone;
Pieire de Maensac is gone.
I have walked over these roads;
I have thought of them living.

CATHAY

FOR THE MOST PART FROM THE CHINESE OF RIHAKU
(LI T'AI PO), FROM THE NOTES OF THE LATE
ERNEST FENOLLOSA, AND THE DECIPHER-
INGS OF THE PROFESSORS MORI
AND ARIGA
(*1915*)

SONG OF THE BOWMEN OF SHU

HERE we are, picking the first fern-shoots
      And saying: When shall we get back to
      our country?
Here we are because we have the Ken-in for our
      foemen,
We have no comfort because of these Mongols.
We grub the soft fern-shoots,
When anyone says "Return," the others are full of
      sorrow.
Sorrowful minds, sorrow is strong, we are hungry
      and thirsty.
Our defence is not yet made sure, no one can let
      his friend return.
We grub the old fern-stalks.
We say: Will we be let to go back in October?
There is no ease in royal affairs, we have no comfort.
Our sorrow is bitter, but we would not return to
      our country.
What flower has come into blossom?
Whose chariot?   The General's.
Horses, his horses even, are tired.   They were
      strong.
We have no rest, three battles a month.
By heaven, his horses are tired.
The generals are on them, the soldiers are by them.
The horses are well trained, the generals have ivory
      arrows and quivers ornamented with fish-skin.
The enemy is swift, we must be careful.
When we set out, the willows were drooping with
      spring,
We come back in the snow,
We go slowly, we are hungry and thirsty,
Our mind is full of sorrow, who will know of our
      grief?

                    Bunno (Shih-ching, 167)

127

THE BEAUTIFUL TOILET

BLUE, blue is the grass about the river
     And the willows have overfilled the close
          garden.
And within, the mistress, in the midmost of her
          youth,
White, white of face, hesitates, passing the door.
Slender, she puts forth a slender hand;

And she was a courtezan in the old days,
And she has married a sot,
Who now goes drunkenly out
And leaves her too much alone.

Attributed to Mei Shêng B.C. 140

THE RIVER SONG

THIS boat is of satō-wood, and its gunwales
          are cut magnolia,
     Musicians with jewelled flutes and with pipes
          of gold
Fill full the sides in rows, and our wine
Is rich for a thousand cups.
We carry singing girls, drift with the drifting water,
Yet Sennin needs
A yellow stork for a charger, and all our seamen
Would follow the white gulls or ride them.
Kutsu's prose song
Hangs with the sun and moon.

King So's terraced palace
          is now but barren hill,
But I draw pen on this barge
Causing the five peaks to tremble,

And I have joy in these words
            like the joy of blue islands.
(If glory could last forever
Then the waters of Han would flow northward.)
              *   *   *
And I have moped in the Emperor's garden, await-
    ing an order-to-write!
I looked at the dragon-pond, with its willow-
    coloured water
Just reflecting the sky's tinge,
And heard the five-score nightingales aimlessly sing-
    ing.

The eastern wind brings the green colour into the
    island grasses at Ei-shū,
The purple house and the crimson are full of Spring
    softness.
South of the pond the willow-tips are half-blue and
    bluer,
Their cords tangle in mist, against the brocade-like
    palace.
Vine-strings a hundred feet long hang down from
    carved railings,
And high over the willows, the fine birds sing to
    each other, and listen,
Crying—"Ken-kwan" for the early wind, and the
    feel of it.
The wind bundles itself into a bluish cloud and wan-
    ders off.
Over a thousand gates, over a thousand doors are
    the sounds of spring singing,
And the Emperor is at Kō.
Five clouds hang aloft, bright on the purple sky,
The imperial guards come forth from the golden
    house with their armour a-gleaming.
The Emperor in his jewelled car goes out to inspect
    his flowers,

He goes out to Hōrai, to look at the wing-flapping
    storks,
He returns by way of Shi rock, to hear the new
    nightingales,
For the gardens at Jō-rin are full of new nightin-
    gales,
Their sound is mixed in this flute,
Their voice is in the twelve pipes here.

By Rihaku (*Li T'ai Po*)
8th century A.D.

THE RIVER-MERCHANT'S WIFE:
A LETTER

WHILE my hair was still cut straight across
        my forehead
            I played about the front gate, pulling
        flowers.
You came by on bamboo stilts, playing horse,
You walked about my seat, playing with blue plums.
And we went on living in the village of Chōkan:
Two small people, without dislike or suspicion.

At fourteen I married My Lord you.
I never laughed, being bashful.
Lowering my head, I looked at the wall.
Called to, a thousand times, I never looked back.

At fifteen I stopped scowling,
I desired my dust to be mingled with yours
Forever and forever and forever.
Why should I climb the look out?

At sixteen you departed,
You went into far Ku-tō-en, by the river of swirl-
    ing eddies,
And you have been gone five months.
The monkeys make sorrowful noise overhead.

You dragged your feet when you went out.
By the gate now, the moss is grown, the different
    mosses,
Too deep to clear them away!
The leaves fall early this autumn, in wind.
The paired butterflies are already yellow with
    August
Over the grass in the West garden;
They hurt me. I grow older.
If you are coming down through the narrows of the
    river Kiang,
Please let me know beforehand,
And I will come out to meet you
                    As far as Chō-fū-Sa.

By Rihaku (Li T'ai Po)

POEM BY THE BRIDGE AT TEN-SHIN

MARCH has come to the bridge head,
    Peach boughs and apricot boughs hang
        over a thousand gates,
At morning there are flowers to cut the heart,
And evening drives them on the eastward-flowing
    waters.
Petals are on the gone waters and on the going,
        And on the back-swirling eddies,
But to-day's men are not the men of the old days,
Though they hang in the same way over the bridge-
    rail.

The sea's colour moves at the dawn
And the princes still stand in rows, about the throne,
And the moon falls over the portals of Sei-jō-yō,
And clings to the walls and the gate-top.
With head gear glittering against the cloud and sun,

The lords go forth from the court, and into far
borders.
They ride upon dragon-like horses,
Upon horses with head-trappings of yellow metal,
And the streets make way for their passage.
Haughty their passing,
Haughty their steps as they go in to great banquets,
To high halls and curious food,
To the perfumed air and girls dancing,
To clear flutes and clear singing;
To the dance of the seventy couples;
To the mad chase through the gardens.
Night and day are given over to pleasure
And they think it will last a thousand autumns,
Unwearying autumns.
For them the yellow dogs howl portents in vain,
And what are they compared to the lady Ryokushu,
That was cause of hate!
Who among them is a man like Han-rei
Who departed alone with his mistress,
With her hair unbound, and he his own skiffsman!

By Rihaku (Li T'ai Po)

THE JEWEL STAIRS' GRIEVANCE

THE jewelled steps are already quite white
with dew,
It is so late that the dew soaks my gauze
stockings,
And I let down the crystal curtain
And watch the moon through the clear autumn.

By Rihaku (Li T'ai Po)

NOTE.—Jewel stairs, therefore a palace. Grievance, therefore
there is something to complain of. Gauze stockings, therefore a
court lady, not a servant who complains. Clear autumn, therefore
she has no excuse on account of weather. Also she has come early,
for the dew has not merely whitened the stairs, but has soaked
her stockings. The poem is especially prized because she utters
no direct reproach.

LAMENT OF THE FRONTIER GUARD

BY the North Gate, the wind blows full of sand,
Lonely from the beginning of time until now!
Trees fall, the grass goes yellow with autumn.
I climb the towers and towers
       to watch out the barbarous land:
Desolate castle, the sky, the wide desert.
There is no wall left to this village.
Bones white with a thousand frosts,
High heaps, covered with trees and grass;
Who brought this to pass?
Who has brought the flaming imperial anger?
Who has brought the army with drums and with
       kettle-drums?
Barbarous kings.
A gracious spring, turned to blood-ravenous autumn,
A turmoil of wars-men, spread over the middle king-
       dom,
Three hundred and sixty thousand,
And sorrow, sorrow like rain.
Sorrow to go, and sorrow, sorrow returning.
Desolate, desolate fields,
And no children of warfare upon them,
       No longer the men for offence and defence.
Ah, how shall you know the dreary sorrow at the
       North Gate,
With Riboku's name forgotten,
And we guardsmen fed to the tigers.

By Rihaku (Li T'ai Po)

EXILE'S LETTER

TŌ So-Kiu of Rakuyō, ancient friend, Chancellor Gen.
    Now I remember that you built me a special tavern
By the south side of the bridge at Ten-shin.
With yellow gold and white jewels, we paid for songs and laughter
And we were drunk for month on month, forgetting the kings and princes.
Intelligent men came drifting in from the sea and from the west border,
And with them, and with you especially
    There was nothing at cross purpose,
And they made nothing of sea-crossing or of mountain-crossing,
If only they could be of that fellowship,
And we all spoke out our hearts and minds, and without regret.
And then I was sent off to South Wai,
    smothered in laurel groves,
And you to the north of Raku-hoku,
Till we had nothing but thoughts and memories in common.
And then, when separation had come to its worst,
We met, and travelled into Sen-jō,
Through all the thirty-six folds of the turning and twisting waters,
Into a valley of the thousand bright flowers,
That was the first valley;
And into ten thousand valleys full of voices and pine-winds.
And with silver harness and reins of gold,
Out came the East of Kan foreman and his company.
And there came also the "True man" of Shi-yō to meet me,

Playing on a jewelled mouth-organ.
In the storied houses of San-ka they gave us more
　　Sennin music,
Many instruments, like the sound of young phœnix
　　broods.
The foreman of Kan-chū, drunk, danced
　　because his long sleeves wouldn't keep still
With that music playing,
And I, wrapped in brocade, went to sleep with my
　　head on his lap,
And my spirit so high it was all over the heavens,
And before the end of the day we were scattered like
　　stars, or rain.
I had to be off to So, far away over the waters,
You back to your river-bridge.

And your father, who was brave as a leopard,
Was governor in Hei Shu, and put down the bar-
　　barian rabble.
And one May he had you send for me,
　　　　despite the long distance.
And what with broken wheels and so on, I won't say
　　it wasn't hard going,
Over roads twisted like sheep's guts.
And I was still going, late in the year,
　　　　in the cutting wind from the North,
And thinking how little you cared for the cost,
　　　　and you caring enough to pay it.
And what a reception:
Red jade cups, food well set on a blue jewelled table,
And I was drunk, and had no thought of returning.
And you would walk out with me to the western
　　corner of the castle,
To the dynastic temple, with water about it clear as
　　blue jade,
With boats floating, and the sound of mouth-organs
　　and drums,

With ripples like dragon-scales, going grass green
    on the water,
Pleasure lasting, with courtezans, going and coming
    without hindrance,
With the willow flakes falling like snow,
And the vermilioned girls getting drunk about sunset,
And the water, a hundred feet deep, reflecting green
    eyebrows
—Eyebrows painted green are a fine sight in young
    moonlight,
Gracefully painted—
And the girls singing back at each other,
Dancing in transparent brocade,
And the wind lifting the song, and interrupting it,
Tossing it up under the clouds.
        And all this comes to an end.
        And is not again to be met with.
I went up to the court for examination,
Tried Yō Yū's luck, offered the Chōyō song,
And got no promotion,
        and went back to the East Mountains
        White-headed.
And once again, later, we met at the South bridge-
    head.
And then the crowd broke up, you went north to
    San palace,
And if you ask how I regret that parting:
It is like the flowers falling at Spring's end
        Confused, whirled in a tangle.
What is the use of talking, and there is no end of
    talking,
There is no end of things in the heart.
I call in the boy,
Have him sit on his knees here
        To seal this,
And send it a thousand miles, thinking.

                       By Rihaku (Li T'ai Po)

FOUR POEMS OF DEPARTURE

Light rain is on the light dust
The willows of the inn-yard
Will be going greener and greener,
But you, Sir, had better take wine ere
    your departure,
For you will have no friends about
    you
When you come to the gates of Yō.
        (Ōmakitsu [Wang Wei])

SEPARATION ON THE RIVER
KIANG

KO-JIN goes west from Kō-kaku-ro,
    The smoke-flowers are blurred over the
    river.
His lone sail blots the far sky.
And now I see only the river,
    The long Kiang, reaching heaven.

                        Rihaku (Li T'ai Po)

TAKING LEAVE OF A FRIEND

BLUE mountains to the north of the walls,
    White river winding about them;
    Here we must make separation
And go out through a thousand miles of dead grass.

Mind like a floating wide cloud,
Sunset like the parting of old acquaintances
Who bow over their clasped hands at a distance.
Our horses neigh to each other
        as we are departing.

                        Rihaku (Li T'ai Po)

137

LEAVE-TAKING NEAR SHOKU

"Sansō, King of Shoku, built roads"

THEY say the roads of Sansō are steep,
Sheer as the mountains.
The walls rise in a man's face,
Clouds grow out of the hill
at his horse's bridle.
Sweet trees are on the paved way of the Shin,
Their trunks burst through the paving,
And freshets are bursting their ice
in the midst of Shoku, a proud city.

Men's fates are already set,
There is no need of asking diviners.

Rihaku (Li T'ai Po)

THE CITY OF CHŌAN

THE phœnix are at play on their terrace.
The phœnix are gone, the river flows on
alone.
Flowers and grass
Cover over the dark path
where lay the dynastic house of the Go.
The bright cloths and bright caps of Shin
Are now the base of old hills.

The Three Mountains fall through the far heaven,
The isle of White Heron
splits the two streams apart.
Now the high clouds cover the sun
And I can not see Chōan afar
And I am sad.

Rihaku (Li T'ai Po)

SOUTH-FOLK IN COLD COUNTRY

THE Dai horse neighs against the bleak wind
        of Etsu,
    The birds of Etsu have no love for En, in
        the north,
Emotion is born out of habit.
Yesterday we went out of the Wild-Goose gate,
To-day from the Dragon-Pen.[1]
Surprised. Desert turmoil. Sea sun.
Flying snow bewilders the barbarian heaven.
Lice swarm like ants over our accoutrements.
Mind and spirit drive on the feathery banners.
Hard fight gets no reward.
Loyalty is hard to explain.
Who will be sorry for General Rishōgun,
        the swift moving,
Whose white head is lost for this province?

[1] *I.e.*, we have been warring from one end of the empire to the
other, now east, now west, on each border.

Rihaku (Li T'ai Po)

SENNIN POEM BY KAKUHAKU (KUO P'U)

THE red and green kingfishers
        flash between the orchids and clover,
    One bird casts its gleam on another.

Green vines hang through the high forest,
They weave a whole roof to the mountain,
The lone man sits with shut speech,
He purrs and pats the clear strings.
He throws his heart up through the sky,
He bites through the flower pistil
        and brings up a fine fountain.
The red-pine-tree god looks at him and wonders.

He rides through the purple smoke to visit the
    sennin,
He takes "Floating Hill"[1] by the sleeve,
He claps his hand on the back of the great water
    sennin.

But you, you dam'd crowd of gnats,
Can you even tell the age of a turtle?

[1] Name of a sennin.

Kakuhaku (*Kuo P'u*)

A BALLAD OF THE MULBERRY
ROAD

THE sun rises in south east corner of things
To look on the tall house of the Shin
For they have a daughter named Rafu,
        (pretty girl)
She made the name for herself: "Gauze Veil,"
For she feeds mulberries to silkworms.
She gets them by the south wall of the town.
With green strings she makes the warp of her
        basket,
She makes the shoulder-straps of her basket
            from the boughs of Katsura,
And she piles her hair up on the left side of her
        head-piece.

Her earrings are made of pearl,
Her underskirt is of green pattern-silk,
Her overskirt is the same silk dyed in purple,
And when men going by look on Rafu
        They set down their burdens,
They stand and twirl their moustaches.

Anon. (*Fenallosa mss., very early*)

OLD IDEA OF CHŌAN BY ROSHŌRIN
(LU CHAO-LIN)

I

THE narrow streets cut into the wide highway
    at Chōan,
    Dark oxen, white horses,
       drag on the seven coaches with outriders.
The coaches are perfumed wood,
The jewelled chair is held up at the crossway,
Before the royal lodge:
A glitter of golden saddles, awaiting the princess;
They eddy before the gate of the barons.
The canopy embroidered with dragons
       drinks in and casts back the sun.
Evening comes.
       The trappings are bordered with mist.
The hundred cords of mist are spread through
       and double the trees,
Night birds, and night women,
Spread out their sounds through the gardens.

II

Birds with flowery wing, hovering butterflies
       crowd over the thousand gates,
Trees that glitter like jade,
       terraces tinged with silver,
The seed of a myriad hues,
A net-work of arbours and passages and covered
Double towers, winged roofs,   [ways,
       border the net-work of ways:
A place of felicitous meeting.
Riō's house stands out on the sky,
       with glitter of colour
As Butei of Kan had made the high golden lotus
       to gather his dews,
Before it another house which I do not know:
How shall we know all the friends
       whom we meet on strange roadways?

Roshōrin (Lu Chao-lin)   141

TO-EM-MEI'S (T'AO CH'IEN) "THE UNMOVING CLOUD"

"Wet springtime," says To-em-mei,
"Wet spring in the garden."

I

THE clouds have gathered, and gathered,
  and the rain falls and falls,
 The eight ply of the heavens
  are all folded into one darkness,
And the wide, flat road stretches out.
I stop in my room toward the East, quiet, quiet,
I pat my new cask of wine.
My friends are estranged, or far distant,
I bow my head and stand still.

II

Rain, rain, and the clouds have gathered,
The eight ply of the heavens are darkness,
The flat land is turned into river.
  "Wine, wine, here is wine!"
I drink by my eastern window.
I think of talking and man,
And no boat, no carriage, approaches.

III

The trees in my east-looking garden
  are bursting out with new twigs,
They try to stir new affection,
And men say the sun and moon keep on moving
  because they can't find a soft seat.

IV

The birds flutter to rest in my tree,
  and I think I have heard them saying,
"It is not that there are no other men
But we like this fellow the best,
But however we long to speak
He can not know of our sorrow."

T'ao Yüan-ming (*T'ao Ch'ien*)
A.D. 365-427

   END OF CATHAY

POEMS
FROM
BLAST
(1914)

SALUTATION THE THIRD

LET us deride the smugness of "The Times": GUFFAW!
  So much for the gagged reviewers,
It will pay them when the worms are wriggling in
  their vitals;
These are they who objected to newness,
Here are their tomb-stones.
   They supported the gag and the ring:
A little BLACK BOX contains them.
   So shall you be also,
You slut-bellied obstructionist,
You sworn foe to free speech and good letters,
You fungus, you continuous gangrene.

Come, let us on with the new deal,
   Let us be done with pandars and jobbery,
Let us spit upon those who pat the big-bellies for
  profit,
Let us go out in the air a bit.

Or perhaps I *will* die at thirty?
Perhaps you will have the pleasure of defiling my
  pauper's grave;
I wish you joy, I proffer you all my assistance.
It has been your habit for long
   to do away with good writers,
You either drive them mad, or else you blink at their
  suicides,
Or else you condone their drugs,
   and talk of insanity and genius,
But I will not go mad to please you,
   I will not flatter you with an early death,
Oh, no, I will stick it out,
   Feel your hates wriggling about my feet
As a pleasant tickle,
   to be observed with derision,

Though many move with suspicion,
          Afraid to say that they hate you;
The taste of my boot?
          Here is the taste of my boot,
Caress it,
          lick off the blacking.

MONUMENTUM AERE, ETC.

YOU say that I take a good deal upon myself;
   That I strut in the robes of assumption.

In a few years no one will remember the *buffo,*
No one will remember the trivial parts of me,
The comic detail will be absent.
As for you, you will rot in the earth,
And it is doubtful if even your manure will be rich
      enough

To keep grass
Over your grave.

COME MY CANTILATIONS

COME my cantilations,
   Let us dump our hatreds into one bunch and
      be done with them,
Hot sun, clear water, fresh wind,
Let me be free of pavements,
Let me be free of the printers.
Let come beautiful people
Wearing raw silk of good colour,
Let come the graceful speakers,
Let come the ready of wit,
Let come the gay of manner, the insolent and the
      exulting.
We speak of burnished lakes,
Of dry air, as clear as metal.

BEFORE SLEEP

1.

THE lateral vibrations caress me,
They leap and caress me,
They work pathetically in my favour,
They seek my financial good.

She of the spear stands present.
The gods of the underworld attend me, O Annubis,
These are they of thy company.
With a pathetic solicitude they attend me;
Undulant,
Their realm is the lateral courses.

2.

Light!
I am up to follow thee, Pallas.
Up and out of their caresses.
You were gone up as a rocket,
Bending your passages from right to left and from
        left to right
In the flat projection of a spiral.
The gods of drugged sleep attend me,
Wishing me well;
I am up to follow thee, Pallas.

POST MORTEM CONSPECTU

A BROWN, fat babe sitting in the lotus,
And you were glad and laughing
With a laughter not of this world.
It is good to splash in the water
And laughter is the end of all things.

FRATRES MINORES

WITH minds still hovering above their testicles
Certain poets here and in France
Still sigh over established and natural fact
Long since fully discussed by Ovid.
They howl. They complain in delicate and exhausted metres
That the twitching of three abdominal nerves
Is incapable of producing a lasting Nirvana.

END OF POEMS FROM BLAST

POEMS
FROM
LUSTRA
(1915)

NEAR PERIGORD

A Perigord, pres del muralh
Tan que i puosch' om gitar ab malh.

YOU'D have men's hearts up from the dust
  And tell their secrets, Messire Cino,
  Right enough? Then read between the lines
    of Uc St. Circ,
Solve me the riddle, for you know the tale.

Bertrans, En Bertrans, left a fine canzone:
"Maent, I love you, you have turned me out.
The voice at Montfort, Lady Agnes' hair,
Bel Miral's stature, the viscountess' throat,
Set all together, are not worthy of you. . . ."
And all the while you sing out that canzone,
Think you that Maent lived at Montagnac,
One at Chalais, another at Malemort
Hard over Brive—for every lady a castle,
Each place strong.

        Oh, *is* it easy enough?
Tairiran held hall in Montagnac,
His brother-in-law was all there was of power
In Perigord, and this good union
Gobbled all the land, and held it later for some
    hundred years.
And our En Bertrans was in Altafort,
Hub of the wheel, the stirrer-up of strife,
As caught by Dante in the last wallow of hell—
The headless trunk "that made its head a lamp,"
For separation wrought out separation,
And he who set the strife between brother and
    brother
And had his way with the old English king,
Viced in such torture for the "counterpass."

How would you live, with neighbours set about you—
Poictiers and Brive, untaken Rochecouart,
Spread like the finger-tips of one frail hand;
And you on that great mountain of a palm—
Not a neat ledge, not Foix between its streams,
But one huge back half-covered up with pine,
Worked for and snatched from the string-purse of
     Born—
The four round towers, four brothers—mostly
     fools:
What could he do but play the desperate chess,
And stir old grudges?
          "Pawn your castles, lords!
Let the Jews pay."
          And the great scene—
(That, maybe, never happened!)
          Beaten at last,
Before the hard old king:
          "Your son, ah, since he died
"My wit and worth are cobwebs brushed aside
"In the full flare of grief. Do what you will."

     Take the whole man, and ravel out the story.
He loved this lady in castle Montagnac?
The castle flanked him—he had need of it.
You read to-day, how long the overlords of Peri-
     gord,
The Talleyrands, have held the place; it was no
     transient fiction.
And Maent failed him? Or saw through the
     scheme?

     And all his net-like thought of new alliance?
Chalais is high, a-level with the poplars.
Its lowest stones just meet the valley tips
Where the low Dronne is filled with water-lilies.
And Rochecouart can match it, stronger yet,

The very spur's end, built on sheerest cliff,
And Malemort keeps its close hold on Brive,
While Born, his own close purse, his rabbit warren,
His subterranean chamber with a dozen doors,
A-bristle with antennæ to feel roads,
To sniff the traffic into Perigord.
And that hard phalanx, that unbroken line,
The ten good miles from there to Maent's castle,
All of his flank—how could he do without her?
And all the road to Cahors, to Toulouse?
What would he do without her?

   "Papiol,
Go forthright singing—Anhes, Cembelins.
There is a throat; ah, there are two white hands;
There is a trellis full of early roses,
And all my heart is bound about with love.
Where am I come with compound flatteries—
What doors are open to fine compliment?"
And every one half jealous of Maent?
He wrote the catch to pit their jealousies
Against her; give her pride in them?

Take his own speech, make what you will of it—
And still the knot, the first knot, of Maent?

   Is it a love poem? Did he sing of war?
Is it an intrigue to run subtly out,
Born of a jongleur's tongue, freely to pass
Up and about and in and out the land,
Mark him a craftsman and a strategist?
(St. Leider had done as much as Polhonac,
Singing a different stave, as closely hidden.)
Oh, there is precedent, legal tradition,
To sing one thing when your song means another,
"*Et albirar ab lor bordon—*"
Foix' count knew that. What is Sir Bertrans'
    singing?

Maent, Maent, and yet again Maent,
Or war and broken heaumes and politics?

II

End fact. Try fiction. Let us say we see
En Bertrans, a tower-room at Hautefort,
Sunset, the ribbon-like road lies, in red cross-light,
Southward toward Montagnac, and he bends at a
    table
Scribbling, swearing between his teeth; by his left
    hand
Lie little strips of parchment covered over,
Scratched and erased with *al* and *ochaisos*.
Testing his list of rhymes, a lean man? Bilious?
With a red straggling beard?
And the green cat's-eye lifts toward Montagnac.

Or take his "magnet" singer setting out,
Dodging his way past Aubeterre, singing at Chalais
    In the vaulted hall,
Or, by a lichened tree at Rochecouart
Aimlessly watching a hawk above the valleys,
Waiting his turn in the mid-summer evening,
Thinking of Aelis, whom he loved heart and
    soul . . .
To find her half alone, Montfort away,
And a brown, placid, hated woman visiting her,
Spoiling his visit, with a year before the next one.
Little enough?
Or carry him forward. "Go through all the courts,
My Magnet," Bertrans had said.

    We came to Ventadour
In the mid love court, he sings out the canzon,
No one hears save Arrimon Luc D'Esparo—
No one hears aught save the gracious sound of com-
    pliments.

Sir Arrimon counts on his fingers, Montfort,
Rochecouart, Chalais, the rest, the tactic,
Malemort, guesses beneath, sends word to Cœur-
de-Lion:
The compact, de Born smoked out, trees felled
About his castle, cattle driven out!
Or no one sees it, and En Bertrans prospered?

And ten years after, or twenty, as you will,
Arnaut and Richard lodge beneath Chalus:
The dull round towers encroaching on the field,
The tents tight drawn, horses at tether
Further and out of reach, the purple night,
The crackling of small fires, the bannerets,
The lazy leopards on the largest banner,
Stray gleams on hanging mail, an armourer's torch-
flare
Melting on steel.

And in the quietest space
They probe old scandals, say de Born is dead;
And we've the gossip (skipped six hundred years).
Richard shall die to-morrow—leave him there
Talking of *trobar clus* with Daniel.
And the "best craftsman" sings out his friend's
song,
Envies its vigour . . . and deplores the technique,
Dispraises his own skill?—That's as you will.
And they discuss the dead man,
Plantagenet puts the riddle: "Did he love her?"
And Arnaut parries: "Did he love your sister?
True, he has praised her, but in some opinion
He wrote that praise only to show he had
The favour of your party; had been well received."

"You knew the man."
        "*You* knew the man."

"I am an artist, you have tried both métiers."
"You were born near him."
            "Do we know our friends?"
"Say that he saw the castles, say that he loved
        Maent!"
"Say that he loved her, does it solve the riddle?"
    End the discussion, Richard goes out next day
And gets a quarrel-bolt shot through his vizard,
Pardons the bowman, dies,

            Ends our discussion.   Arnaut ends
"In sacred odour"—(that's apocryphal!)
And we can leave the talk till Dante writes:
Surely I saw, and still before my eyes
Goes on that headless trunk, that bears for light
Its own head swinging, gripped by the dead hair,
And like a swinging lamp that says, "Ah me!
I severed men, my head and heart
Ye see here severed, my life's counterpart."

Or take En Bertrans?

III

Ed eran due in uno, ed uno in due;
Inferno, XXVIII, 125

BEWILDERING spring, and by the Auvezere
    Poppies and day's eyes in the green émail
    Rose over us; and we knew all that stream,
And our two horses had traced out the valleys;
Knew the low flooded lands squared out with
    poplars,
In the young days when the deep sky befriended.
    And great wings beat above us in the
    twilight,
And the great wheels in heaven
Bore us together . . . surging . . . and apart . . .
Believing we should meet with lips and hands,

   High, high and sure . . . and then the counter-
    thrust:
'Why do you love me? Will you always love me?
But I am like the grass, I can not love you.'
Or, 'Love, and I love and love you,
And hate your mind, not *you,* your soul, your hands.'

   So to this last estrangement, Tairiran!

   There shut up in his castle, Tairiran's,
She who had nor ears nor tongue save in her
    hands,
Gone—ah, gone—untouched, unreachable!
She who could never live save through one person,
She who could never speak save to one person,
And all the rest of her a shifting change,
A broken bundle of mirrors . . . !

VILLANELLE: THE PSYCHOLOGICAL HOUR

I HAD over-prepared the event,
    that much was ominous.
With middle-ageing care
    I had laid out just the right books.
I had almost turned down the pages.

    Beauty is so rare a thing.
    So few drink of my fountain.

So much barren regret,
So many hours wasted!
And now I watch, from the window,
    the rain, the wandering busses.

"Their little cosmos is shaken"—
    the air is alive with that fact.
In their parts of the city
    they are played on by diverse forces.
How do I know?
    Oh, I know well enough.
For them there is something afoot.
    As for me;
I had over-prepared the event—

    Beauty is so rare a thing
    So few drink of my fountain.

Two friends: a breath of the forest . . .
Friends? Are people less friends
    because one has just, at last, found them?
Twice they promised to come.

    "Between the night and morning?"

Beauty would drink of my mind.
Youth would awhile forget
    my youth is gone from me.

II

("Speak up! You have danced so stiffly?
Someone admired your works,
And said so frankly.

"Did you talk like a fool,
The first night?
The second evening?"

"*But* they promised again:
'To-morrow at tea-time.' ")

III

Now the third day is here—
no word from either;
No word from her nor him,
Only another man's note:
"Dear Pound, I am leaving England."

DANS UN OMNIBUS DE LONDRES

LES yeux d'une morte
   M'ont salué,
     Enchassés dans un visage stupide
Dont tous les autres traits étaient banals,
Ils m'ont salué
Et alors je vis bien des choses
Au dedans de ma mémoire
Remuer,
S'éveiller.

Je vis des canards sur le bord d'un lac minuscule,
Auprès d'un petit enfant gai, bossu.

Je vis les colonnes anciennes en "toc"
Du Parc Monceau,
Et deux petites filles graciles,
Des patriciennes,
         aux toisons couleur de lin,
Et des pigeonnes
Grasses
       comme des poulardes.
Je vis le parc,
Et tous les gazons divers
Où nous avions loué des chaises
Pour quatre sous.

Je vis les cygnes noirs,
Japonais,
Leurs ailes
Teintées de couleur sang-de-dragon,
Et toutes les fleurs
D'Armenonville.

Les yeux d'une morte
M'ont salué.

PAGANI'S, NOVEMBER 8

SUDDENLY discovering in the eyes of the
very beautiful
Normande cocotte
The eyes of the very learned British Museum as-
sistant.

TO A FRIEND WRITING ON
CABARET DANCERS

"Breathe not the word to-morrow in her ears"
Vir Quidem, on Dancers

GOOD "Hedgethorn," for we'll anglicize
your name
Until the last slut's hanged and the last
pig disemboweled,
Seeing your wife is charming and your child
Sings in the open meadow—at least the kodak says
so—

My good fellow, you, on a cabaret silence
And the dancers, you write a sonnet;

Say "Forget To-morrow," being of all men
The most prudent, orderly, and decorous!

"Pepita" has no to-morrow, so you write.

Pepita has such to-morrows: with the hands puffed
out,
The pug-dog's features encrusted with tallow
Sunk in a frowsy collar—an unbrushed black.
She will not bathe too often, but her jewels
Will be a stuffy, opulent sort of fungus
Spread on both hands and on the up-pushed-bosom—
It juts like a shelf between the jowl and corset.
Have you, or I, seen most of cabarets, good Hedge-
thorn?

Here's Pepita, tall and slim as an Egyptian mummy,
Marsh-cranberries, the ribbed and angular pods
Flare up with scarlet orange on stiff stalks
And so Pepita
Flares on the crowded stage before our tables
Or slithers about between the dishonest waiters—

> "CARMEN EST MAIGRE, UN TRAIT DE BISTRE
> CERNE SON ŒIL DE GITANA"

And "rend la flamme",
            you know the deathless verses.
I search the features, the avaricious features
Pulled by the kohl and rouge out of resemblance—
Six pence the object for a change of passion.

"Write me a poem."
            Come now, my dear Pepita,
"-ita, bonita, chiquita,"
That's what you mean you advertising spade,
Or take the intaglio, my fat great-uncle's heirloom:
Cupid, astride a phallus with two wings,
Swinging a cat-o'-nine-tails.
                No. Pepita,
I have seen through the crust.
                I don't know what you look like
But your smile pulls one way
                and your painted grin another,
While that cropped fool,
                that tom-boy who can't earn her living,
Come, come to-morrow,
                To-morrow in ten years at the latest,
She will be drunk in the ditch, but you, Pepita,
Will be quite rich, quite plump, with pug-bitch
        features,
With a black tint staining your cuticle,
Prudent and svelte Pepita.
                "Poète, writ me a poème!"

Spanish and Paris, love of the arts part of your
  geisha-culture!
Euhenia, in short skirts, slaps her wide stomach,
Pulls up a roll of fat for the pianist,
"Pauvre femme maigre!" she says.
    He sucks his chop bone,
That some one else has paid for,
   grins up an amiable grin,
Explains the decorations.
    Good Hedgethorn, they all have futures,
All these people.
    Old Popkoff
Will dine next week with Mrs. Basil,
Will meet a duchess and an ex-diplomat's widow
From Weehawken—who has never known
Any but "Majesties" and Italian nobles.
Euhenia will have a *fonda* in Orbajosa.
The amorous nerves will give way to digestive;
"Delight thy soul in fatness," saith the preacher.
We can't preserve the elusive *"mica salis,"*
It may last well in these dark northern climates,
Nell Gwynn's still here, despite the reformation,
And Edward's mistresses still light the stage,
A glamour of classic youth in their deportment.
The prudent whore is not without her future,
Her bourgeois dulness is deferred.

    Her present dulness . . .
Oh well, her present dulness . . .
Now in Venice, 'Storante al Giardino, I went early,
Saw the performers come: him, her, the baby,
A quiet and respectable-tawdry trio;
An hour later: a show of calves and spangles,
"Un e duo fanno tre,"
    Night after night,
No change, no change of program, *"Che!*
"La donna è mobile."

HOMAGE TO QUINTUS SEPTIMIUS
FLORENS CHRISTIANUS

(Ex libris Graecæ)

I

THEODORUS will be pleased at my death,
And someone else will be pleased at the
death of Theodorus,
And yet everyone speaks evil of death.

II

This place is the Cyprian's for she has ever the
fancy
To be looking out across the bright sea,
Therefore the sailors are cheered, and the waves
Keep small with reverence, beholding her image.

Anyte

III

A sad and great evil is the expectation of death—
And there are also the inane expenses of the
funeral;
Let us therefore cease from pitying the dead
For after death there comes no other calamity.

Palladas

IV

Troy

Whither, O city, are your profits and your gilded
     shrines,
And your barbecues of great oxen,
And the tall women walking your streets, in gilt
     clothes,
With their perfumes in little alabaster boxes?
Where is the work of your home-born sculptors?

Time's tooth is into the lot, and war's and fate's
     too.
Envy has taken your all,
Save your douth and your story.

Agathias Scholasticus

V

Woman? Oh, woman is a consummate rage,
     but dead, or asleep, she pleases.
Take her. She has two excellent seasons.

Palladas

VI

Nicarchus upon Phidon his doctor

Phidon neither purged me, nor touched me,
But I remembered the name of his fever medicine
     and died.

FISH AND THE SHADOW

THE salmon-trout drifts in the stream,
  The soul of the salmon-trout floats over the
    stream
      Like a little wafer of light.

The salmon moves in the sun-shot, bright shallow
    sea. . . .

As light as the shadow of the fish
              that falls through the water,
She came into the large room by the stair,
Yawning a little she came with the sleep still upon
    her.

"I am just from bed. The sleep is still in my eyes.
"Come. I have had a long dream."
And I: "That wood?
"And two springs have passed us."
"Not so far, no, not so far now,
There is a place—but no one else knows it—
A field in a valley . . .
                        Qu'ieu sui avinen,
Ieu lo sai."

She must speak of the time
Of Arnaut de Mareuil, I thought, *"qu'ieu sui
    avinen."*

Light as the shadow of the fish
That falls through the pale green water.

IMPRESSIONS OF FRANÇOIS-MARIE AROUET (DE VOLTAIRE)

I

Phyllidula and the Spoils of Gouvernet

WHERE, Lady, are the days
　　When you could go out in a hired hansom
　　Without footmen and equipments?
And dine in a soggy, cheap restaurant?
Phyllidula now, with your powdered Swiss footman
Clanking the door shut,
　　　　and lying;
And carpets from Savonnier, and from Persia,
And your new service at dinner,
And plates from Germain,
And cabinets and chests from Martin (almost lac-
　　quer),
And your white vases from Japan,
And the lustre of diamonds,
Etcetera, etcetera, and etcetera?

II

To Madame du Châtelet

If you'd have me go on loving you
Give me back the time of the thing.

Will you give me dawn light at evening?
Time has driven me out from the fine plaisaunces,
The parks with the swards all over dew,
And grass going glassy with the light on it,
The green stretches where love is and the grapes
Hang in yellow-white and dark clusters ready for
　　pressing.

And if now we can't fit with our time of life
There is not much but its evil left us.

Life gives us two minutes, two seasons—
        One to be dull in;
Two deaths—and to stop loving and being lovable,
That is the real death,
The other is little beside it.

Crying after the follies gone by me,
Quiet talking is all that is left us—
Gentle talking, not like the first talking, less lively;
And to follow after friendship, as they call it,
Weeping that we can follow naught else.

III

To Madame Lullin

You'll wonder that an old man of eighty
Can go on writing you verses. . . .

Grass showing under the snow,
Birds singing late in the year!

And Tibullus could say of his death, in his Latin:
"Delia, I would look on you, dying."

And Delia herself fading out,
Forgetting even her beauty.

END OF LUSTRA

PHANOPOEIA

I

ROSE WHITE, YELLOW, SILVER

THE swirl of light follows me through the
    square,
The smoke of incense
Mounts from the four horns of my bed-posts,
The water-jet of gold light bears us up through the
    ceilings;
Lapped in the gold-coloured flame I descend through
    the æther.
The silver ball forms in my hand,
It falls and rolls to your feet.

II

SALTUS

The swirling sphere has opened
    and you are caught up to the skies,
You are englobed in my sapphire.
                 Io! Io!

You have perceived the blades of the flame
The flutter of sharp-edged sandals.

The folding and lapping brightness
Has held in the air before you.
You have perceived the leaves of the flame.

III

The wire-like bands of colour involute mount from
    my fingers;
I have wrapped the wind round your shoulders
And the molten metal of your shoulders
    bends into the turn of the wind,

AOI!
The whirling tissue of light
    is woven and grows solid beneath us;
The sea-clear sapphire of air, the sea-dark clarity,
    stretches both sea-cliff and ocean.

LANGUE D'OC

Alba

WHEN the nightingale to his mate
Sings day-long and night late
My love and I keep state
In bower,
In flower,
'Till the watchman on the tower
Cry:

> *"Up! Thou rascal, Rise,*
> *I see the white*
> *Light*
> *And the night*
> *Flies."*

I

Compleynt of a gentleman who has been waiting outside for some time

O PLASMATOUR and true celestial light,
　　Lord powerful, engirdlèd all with might,
　　Give my good-fellow aid in fools' despite
Who stirs not forth this night,
　　　　　　　　　And day comes on.
"Sst! my good fellow, art awake or sleeping?
Sleep thou no more.　I see the star upleaping
That hath the dawn in keeping,
　　　　　　　　　And day comes on!
"Hi!　Harry, hear me, for I sing aright
Sleep not thou now, I hear the bird in flight
That plaineth of the going of the night,
　　　　　　　　　And day comes on!
"Come now!　Old swenkin!　Rise up from thy bed,
I see the signs upon the welkin spread,
If thou come not, the cost be on thy head.
　　　　　　　　　And day comes on!
"And here I am since going down of sun,
And pray to God that is St. Mary's son,
To bring thee safe back, my companion.
　　　　　　　　　And day comes on.
"And thou out here beneath the porch of stone
Badest me to see that a good watch was done,
And now thou'lt none of me, and wilt have none
　　　　　　　　　Of song of mine."

(Bass voice from inside.)

"Wait, my good fellow.　For such joy I take
With her venust and noblest to my make
To hold embracèd, and will not her forsake
For yammer of the cuckold,
　　　　　　　　　Though day break."
　　　　　　　　　(Girart Bornello.)

II

Avril

WHEN the springtime is sweet
    And the birds repeat
      Their new song in the leaves.
'Tis meet
A man go where he will.

But from where my heart is set
No message I get;
My heart all wakes and grieves;
Defeat
Or luck, I must have my fill.

Our love comes out
Like the branch that turns about
On the top of the hawthorne,
With frost and hail at night
Suffers despite
'Till the sun come, and the green leaf on the bough.

I remember the young day
When we set strife away,
And she gave me such gesning,
Her love and her ring:
God grant I die not by any man's stroke
'Till I have my hand 'neath her cloak.

I care not for their clamour
Who have come between me and my charmer,
For I know how words run loose,
Big talk and little use.
Spoilers of pleasure,
We take their measure.

(*Guilhem de Peitieu.*)

III

Descant on a Theme by Cerclamon

WHEN the sweet air goes bitter,
    And the cold birds twitter
    Where the leaf falls from the twig,
I sough and sing

      that Love goes out
    Leaving me no power to hold him.

Of love I have naught
Save trouble and sad thought,
And nothing is grievous
      as I desirous,
Wanting only what
No man can get or has got.

With the noblest that stands in men's sight,
If all the world be in despite
      I care not a glove.
Where my love is, there is a glitter of sun;
God give me life, and let my course run

      'Till I have her I love
      To lie with and prove.

I do not live, nor cure me,
Nor feel my ache—great as it is,
For love will give
      me no respite,
Nor do I know when I turn left or right
      nor when I go out.

      For in her is all my delight
      And all that can save me.

I shake and burn and quiver
From love, awake and in swevyn,
Such fear I have she deliver
                    me not from pain,
          Who know not how to ask her;
          Who can not.
Two years, three years I seek
And though I fear to speak out,
          Still she must know it.

If she won't have me now, Death is my portion,
          Would I had died that day
          I came into her sway.
God! How softly this kills!
When her love look steals on me.
Killed me she has, I know not how it was,
          For I would not look on a woman.

Joy I have none, if she make me not mad
          Or set me quiet, or bid me chatter.
Good is it to me if she flout
          Or turn me inside out, and about.
          My ill doth she turn sweet.

How swift it is.
          For I am traist and loose,
          I am true, or a liar,
          All vile, or all gentle,
          Or shaking between,
                    as she desire,
I, Cerclamon, sorry and glad,
          The man whom love had
                    and has ever;
          Alas! who'er it please or pain,
          She can me retain.

I am gone from one joy,
From one I loved never so much,
    She by one touch
    Reft me away;
    So doth bewilder me
    I can not say my say

                nor my desire,
    And when she looks on me
    It seems to me
            I lose all wit and sense.

    The noblest girls men love
    'Gainst her I prize not as a glove
    Worn and old.
    Though the whole world run rack
    And go dark with cloud,
    Light is
    Where she stands,
    And a clamour loud

            in my ears.

IV

Vergier

IN orchard under the hawthorne
She has her lover till morn,
   Till the traist man cry out to warn
Them. God how swift the night,
               And day comes on.

O Plasmatour, that thou end not the night,
Nor take my belovèd from my sight,
Nor I, nor tower-man, look on daylight,
'Fore God, How swift the night,
               And day comes on.

"Lovely thou art, to hold me close and kisst,
  Now cry the birds out, in the meadow mist,
  Despite the cuckold, do thou as thou list,
  So swiftly goes the night
               And day comes on.

"My pretty boy, make we our play again
  Here in the orchard where the birds complain,
  'Till the traist watcher his song unrein,
  Ah God! How swift the night
               And day comes on."

"Out of the wind that blows from her,
  That dancing and gentle is and thereby pleasanter,
  Have I drunk a draught, sweeter than scent of
      myrrh.
Ah God! How swift the night.
               And day comes on."

Venust the lady, and none lovelier,
For her great beauty, many men look on her,
Out of my love will her heart not stir.
By God, how swift the night.
               And day comes on.

MOEURS CONTEMPORAINES

I

Mr. Styrax   1

MR. HECATOMB STYRAX, the owner of
     a large estate
                         and of large muscles,
A "blue" and a climber of mountains, has married
                         at the age of 28,
He being at that age a virgin,
The term "virgo" being made male in mediaeval
     latinity;
                    His ineptitudes
Have driven his wife from one religious excess to
     another.
She has abandoned the vicar
For he was lacking in vehemence;
She is now the high-priestess
Of a modern and ethical cult,
                    And even now Mr. Styrax
                    Does not believe in aesthetics.

                              2

His brother has taken to gipsies,
But the son-in-law of Mr. H. Styrax
Objects to perfumed cigarettes.
                    In the parlance of Niccolo Machiavelli:
                    "Thus things proceed in their circle";
                    And thus the empire is maintained.

II

Clara

AT sixteen she was a potential celebrity
With a distaste for caresses.
She now writes to me from a convent;
Her life is obscure and troubled;
Her second husband will not divorce her;
Her mind is, as ever, uncultivated,
And no issue presents itself.
She does not desire her children,
Or any more children.
Her ambition is vague and indefinite,
She will neither stay in, nor come out.

III

Soirée

UPON learning that the mother wrote verses,
And that the father wrote verses,
And that the youngest son was in a publisher's
office,
And that the friend of the second daughter was
undergoing a novel,
The young American pilgrim
Exclaimed:
"This is a darn'd clever bunch!"

IV

Sketch 48 b. 11

AT the age of 27
Its home mail is still opened by its maternal
parent
And its office mail may be opened by
its parent of the opposite gender.
It is an officer,
and a gentleman,
and an architect.

V

I

AT a friend of my wife's there is a photograph,
A faded, pale brownish photograph,
   Of the times when the sleeves were large,
Silk, stiff and large above the *lacertus,*
That is, the upper arm,
And décolleté. . . .
                     It is a lady,
She sits at a harp,
Playing,

And by her left foot, in a basket,
Is an infant, aged about 14 months,
The infant beams at the parent,
The parent re-beams at its offspring.
The basket is lined with satin,
There is a satin-like bow on the harp.

2

And in the home of the novelist
There is a satin-like bow on an harp.
You enter and pass hall after hall,
Conservatory follows conservatory,
Lilies lift their white symbolical cups,
Whence their symbolical pollen has been excerpted,
Near them I noticed an harp
And the blue satin ribbon,
And the copy of "Hatha Yoga"
And the neat piles of unopened, unopening books,

And she spoke to me of the monarch,
And of the purity of her soul.

VI

Stele

AFTER years of continence
  he hurled himself into a sea of six women.
    Now, quenched as the brand of Meleagar,
      he lies by the poluphloisboious sea-coast.

Παρὰ θῖνα πολυφλοίσβοιο θαλάσσης.

SISTE VIATOR.

VII

I Vecchii

THEY will come no more,
  The old men with beautiful manners.

Il était comme un tout petit garçon
With his blouse full of apples
And sticking out all the way round;
Blagueur! "Con gli occhi onesti e tardi,"

And he said:
      "Oh! Abelard!" as if the topic
Were much too abstruse for his comprehension,
And he talked about "the Great Mary,"
And said: "Mr. Pound is shocked at my levity."
When it turned out he meant Mrs. Ward.

And the other was rather like my bust by Gaudier,
Or like a real Texas colonel,
He said: "Why flay dead horses?
"There was once a man called Voltaire."

181

And he said they used to cheer Verdi.
In Rome, after the opera,
And the guards couldn't stop them,

And that was an anagram for Vittorio
Emanuele Re D' Italia,
And the guards couldn't stop them.

Old men with beautiful manners,
Sitting in the Row of a morning;
Walking on the Chelsea Embankment.

VIII

Ritratto

AND she said:
         "You remember Mr. Lowell,
    "He was your ambassador here?"
And I said: "That was before I arrived."
And she said:
             "He stomped into my bedroom. . . .
(By that time she had got on to Browning.)
". . . stomped into my bedroom. . . .
"And said: 'Do I,
" 'I ask you, Do I
" 'Care too much for society dinners?'
"And I wouldn't say that he didn't.
"Shelley used to live in this house."

She was a very old lady,
I never saw her again.

CANTICO DEL SOLE[1]

(From "Instigations")

THE thought of what America would be like
    If the Classics had a wide circulation
        Troubles my sleep,
The thought of what America,
The thought of what America,
The thought of what America would be like
If the Classics had a wide circulation
        Troubles my sleep.
Nunc dimittis, now lettest thou thy servant,
Now lettest thou thy servant
        Depart in peace.
The thought of what America,
The thought of what America,
The thought of what America would be like
If the Classics had a wide circulation . . .
        Oh well!
        It troubles my sleep.

---

[1] NOTE FOR "CANTICO DEL SOLE"

This poem formed the conclusion of Pound's essay "The Classics 'Escape'," printed originally in the *Little Review* for March 1918 and collected in *Instigations* (1920). (The poem as printed in *Instigations* is followed by the Latin *"Oravimus"* [we have prayed]). In that essay Pound had printed Section 211 of the United States Criminal Code—on obscene publications—and quoted a recent decision from "a learned judge" that some

> *approved publications at times escape [the law] only be-cause they come within the term "classics," which means, for the purpose of the application of the statute, that they are ordinarily immune from interference, because they have the sanction of age and fame and USUALLY AP-PEAL TO A COMPARATIVELY LIMITED NUMBER OF READERS* [Pound's capitals].

The idea that "Our literature . . . is subject to the taste of one individual . . . selected without any examination of his literary qualifications" outraged Pound; but he considered the matter far too serious to be written of in anger. Instead he expressed his feelings in the cadences of the "Cantico del Sole" of St. Francis of Assisi. For Pound's version of the Italian original see *The Spirit of Romance* (1910), pp. 88–89. —DONALD GALLUP

HUGH SELWYN MAUBERLEY

(LIFE AND CONTACTS)

The sequence is so distinctly a farewell to London that the reader who chooses to regard this as an exclusively American edition may as well omit it and turn at once to page 205.

"VOCAT ÆSTUS IN UMBRAM"
Nemesianus, Ec. IV.

E. P. ODE POUR L'ELECTION DE SON SEPULCHRE

I

FOR three years, out of key with his time,
He strove to resuscitate the dead art
Of poetry; to maintain "the sublime"
In the old sense. Wrong from the start—

No, hardly, but seeing he had been born
In a half savage country, out of date;
Bent resolutely on wringing lilies from the acorn;
Capaneus; trout for factitious bait;

Ἴδμεν γάρ τοι πάνθ', ὅσ' ἐνὶ Τροίῃ
Caught in the unstopped ear;
Giving the rocks small lee-way
The chopped seas held him, therefore, that year.

His true Penelope was Flaubert,
He fished by obstinate isles;
Observed the elegance of Circe's hair
Rather than the mottoes on sun-dials.

Unaffected by "the march of events,"
He passed from men's memory in *l'an trentuniesme
De son eage;* the case presents
No adjunct to the Muses' diadem.

THE age demanded an image
   Of its accelerated grimace,
   Something for the modern stage,
Not, at any rate, an Attic grace;

Not, not certainly, the obscure reveries
Of the inward gaze;
Better mendacities *falsehoods*
Than the classics in paraphrase!

The "age demanded" chiefly a mould in plaster,
Made with no loss of time,
A prose kinema, not, not assuredly, alabaster *translucent mineral*
Or the "sculpture" of rhyme.

III

THE tea-rose tea-gown, etc.
　　Supplants the mousseline of Cos,
　　The pianola "replaces"
Sappho's barbitos.

Christ follows Dionysus,
Phallic and ambrosial
Made way for macerations;
Caliban casts out Ariel.

All things are a flowing,
Sage Heracleitus says;
But a tawdry cheapness
Shall outlast our days.

Even the Christian beauty
Defects—after Samothrace;
We see τὸ καλόν
Decreed in the market place.

Faun's flesh is not to us,
Nor the saint's vision.
We have the press for wafer;
Franchise for circumcision.

All men, in law, are equals.
Free of Pisistratus,
We choose a knave or an eunuch
To rule over us.

O bright Apollo,
τίν᾽ ἄνδρα, τίν᾽ ἥρωα, τινα θεόν,
What god, man, or hero
Shall I place a tin wreath upon!

THESE fought in any case,
   and   some believing,
                   pro domo, in any case . . .

Some quick to arm,
some for adventure,
some from fear of weakness,
some from fear of censure,
some for love of slaughter, in imagination,
learning later . . .
some in fear, learning love of slaughter;

Died some, pro patria,
            non "dulce" non "et decor" . . .
walked eye-deep in hell
believing in old men's lies, then unbelieving
came home, home to a lie,
home to many deceits,
home to old lies and new infamy;
usury age-old and age-thick
and liars in public places.

Daring as never before, wastage as never before.
Young blood and high blood,
fair cheeks, and fine bodies;

fortitude as never before

frankness as never before,
disillusions as never told in the old days,
hysterias, trench confessions,
laughter out of dead bellies.

THERE died a myriad,
  And of the best, among them,
  For an old bitch gone in the teeth,
For a botched civilization,

Charm, smiling at the good mouth,
Quick eyes gone under earth's lid,

For two gross of broken statues,
For a few thousand battered books.

YEUX GLAUQUES

GLADSTONE was still respected,
When John Ruskin produced
"Kings' Treasuries"; Swinburne
And Rossetti still abused.

Fœtid Buchanan lifted up his voice
When that faun's head of hers
Became a pastime for
Painters and adulterers.

The Burne-Jones cartons
Have preserved her eyes;
Still, at the Tate, they teach
Cophetua to rhapsodize;

Thin like brook-water,
With a vacant gaze.
The English Rubaiyat was still-born
In those days.

The thin, clear gaze, the same
Still darts out faun-like from the half-ruin'd face,
Questing and passive. . . .
"Ah, poor Jenny's case" . . .

Bewildered that a world
Shows no surprise
At her last maquero's
Adulteries.

"SIENA MI FE'; DISFECEMI MAREMMA"

AMONG the pickled fœtuses and bottled bones,
 Engaged in perfecting the catalogue,
  I found the last scion of the
Senatorial families of Strasbourg, Monsieur Verog.

For two hours he talked of Galliffet;
Of Dowson; of the Rhymers' Club;
Told me how Johnson (Lionel) died
By falling from a high stool in a pub . . .

But showed no trace of alcohol
At the autopsy, privately performed—
Tissue preserved—the pure mind
Arose toward Newman as the whiskey warmed.

Dowson found harlots cheaper than hotels;
Headlam for uplift; Image impartially imbued
With raptures for Bacchus, Terpsichore and the
  Church.
So spoke the author of "The Dorian Mood,"

M. Verog, out of step with the decade,
Detached from his contemporaries,
Neglected by the young,
Because of these reveries.

BRENNBAUM

THE sky-like limpid eyes,
 The circular infant's face,
  The stiffness from spats to collar
Never relaxing into grace;

The heavy memories of Horeb, Sinai and the forty
  years,
Showed only when the daylight fell
Level across the face
Of Brennbaum "The Impeccable."

MR. NIXON

IN the cream gilded cabin of his steam yacht
   Mr. Nixon advised me kindly, to advance with
     fewer
Dangers of delay. "Consider
     "Carefully the reviewer.

"I was as poor as you are;
"When I began I got, of course,
"Advance on royalties, fifty at first," said Mr.
     Nixon,
"Follow me, and take a column,
"Even if you have to work free.

"Butter reviewers. From fifty to three hundred
"I rose in eighteen months;
"The hardest nut I had to crack
"Was Dr. Dundas.

"I never mentioned a man but with the view
"Of selling my own works.
"The tip's a good one, as for literature
"It gives no man a sinecure.

"And no one knows, at sight, a masterpiece.
"And give up verse, my boy,
"There's nothing in it."

.   .   .   .

Likewise a friend of Blougram's once advised me:
Don't kick against the pricks,
Accept opinion. The "Nineties" tried your game
And died, there's nothing in it.

X

BENEATH the sagging roof
The stylist has taken shelter,
Unpaid, uncelebrated,
At last from the world's welter

Nature receives him;
With a placid and uneducated mistress
He exercises his talents
And the soil meets his distress.

The haven from sophistications and contentions
Leaks through its thatch;
He offers succulent cooking;
The door has a creaking latch.

XI

"CONSERVATRIX of Milésien"
Habits of mind and feeling,
Possibly. But in Ealing
With the most bank-clerkly of Englishmen?

No, "Milésian" is an exaggeration.
No instinct has survived in her
Older than those her grandmother
Told her would fit her station.

"DAPHNE with her thighs in bark
Stretches toward me her leafy hands,"—
Subjectively. In the stuffed-satin drawing-
room
I await The Lady Valentine's commands,

Knowing my coat has never been
Of precisely the fashion
To stimulate, in her,
A durable passion;

Doubtful, somewhat, of the value
Of well-gowned approbation
Of literary effort,
But never of The Lady Valentine's vocation:

Poetry, her border of ideas,
The edge, uncertain, but a means of blending
With other strata
Where the lower and higher have ending;

A hook to catch the Lady Jane's attention,
A modulation toward the theatre,
Also, in the case of revolution,
A possible friend and comforter.

.   .   .   .

Conduct, on the other hand, the soul
"Which the highest cultures have nourished"
To Fleet St. where
Dr. Johnson flourished;

Beside this thoroughfare
The sale of half-hose has
Long since superseded the cultivation
Of Pierian roses.

ENVOI (1919)

Go, dumb-born book,
   Tell her that sang me once that song of
        Lawes:
Hadst thou but song
As thou hast subjects known,
Then were there cause in thee that should condone
Even my faults that heavy upon me lie,
And build her glories their longevity.

Tell her that sheds
Such treasure in the air,
Recking naught else but that her graces give
Life to the moment,
I would bid them live
As roses might, in magic amber laid,
Red overwrought with orange and all made
One substance and one colour
Braving time.

Tell her that goes
With song upon her lips
But sings not out the song, nor knows
The maker of it, some other mouth,
May be as fair as hers,
Might, in new ages, gain her worshippers,
When our two dusts with Waller's shall be laid,
Siftings on siftings in oblivion,
Till change hath broken down
All things save Beauty alone.

MAUBERLEY

1920

"Vacuos exercet in aera morsus."

I

TURNED from the "eau-forte
 Par Jacquemart"
 To the strait head
Of Messalina:

"His true Penelope
Was Flaubert,"
And his tool
The engraver's.

Firmness,
Not the full smile,
His art, but an art
In profile;

Colourless
Pier Francesca,
Pisanello lacking the skill
To forge Achaia.

II

*"Qu'est ce qu'ils savent de l'amour, et
qu'est ce qu'ils peuvent en comprendre?*

*S'ils ne comprennent pas la poésie,
s'ils ne sentent pas la musique, qu'est ce
qu'ils peuvent comprendre de cette pas-
sion en comparaison avec laquelle la rose
est grossière et le parfum des violettes un
tonnerre?"*   CAID ALI

FOR three years, diabolus in the scale,
   He drank ambrosia,
      All passes, ANANGKE prevails,
Came end, at last, to that Arcadia.

He had moved amid her phantasmagoria,
Amid her galaxies,
NUKTOS 'AGALMA

.   .   .   .

Drifted . . . drifted precipitate,
Asking time to be rid of . . .
Of his bewilderment; to designate
His new found orchid. . . .

To be certain . . . certain . . .
(Amid ærial flowers) . . . time for arrangements—
Drifted on
To the final estrangement;

Unable in the supervening blankness
To sift TO AGATHON from the chaff
Until he found his sieve . . .
Ultimately, his seismograph:

—Given that is his "fundamental passion,"
This urge to convey the relation
Of eye-lid and cheek-bone
By verbal manifestation;

To present the series
Of curious heads in medallion—

He had passed, inconscient, full gaze,
The wide-banded irides
And botticellian sprays implied
In their diastasis;

Which anæthesis, noted a year late,
And weighed, revealed his great affect,
(Orchid), mandate
Of Eros, a retrospect.

.   .   .

Mouths biting empty air,
The still stone dogs,
Caught in metamorphosis, were
Left him as epilogues.

"THE AGE DEMANDED"

Vide Poem II. Page 188

FOR this agility chance found
Him of all men, unfit
As the red-beaked steeds of
The Cytheræan for a chain bit.

The glow of porcelain
Brought no reforming sense
To his perception
Of the social inconsequence.

Thus, if her colour
Came against his gaze,
Tempered as if
It were through a perfect glaze

He made no immediate application
Of this to relation of the state
To the individual, the month was more temperate
Because this beauty had been.

> The coral isle, the lion-coloured sand
> Burst in upon the porcelain revery:
> Impetuous troubling
> Of his imagery.

Mildness, amid the neo-Nietzschean clatter,
His sense of graduations,
Quite out of place amid
Resistance to current exacerbations,

Invitation, mere invitation to perceptivity
Gradually led him to the isolation
Which these presents place
Under a more tolerant, perhaps, examination.

By constant elimination
The manifest universe
Yielded an armour
Against utter consternation,

A Minoan undulation,
Seen, we admit, amid ambrosial circumstances
Strengthened him against
The discouraging doctrine of chances,

And his desire for survival,
Faint in the most strenuous moods,
Became an Olympian *apathein*
In the presence of selected perceptions.

A pale gold, in the aforesaid pattern,
The unexpected palms
Destroying, certainly, the artist's urge,
Left him delighted with the imaginary
Audition of the phantasmal sea-surge,

Incapable of the least utterance or composition,
Emendation, conservation of the "better tradition,"
Refinement of medium, elimination of superfluities,
August attraction or concentration.

Nothing, in brief, but maudlin confession,
Irresponse to human aggression,
Amid the precipitation, down-float
Of insubstantial manna,
Lifting the faint susurrus
Of his subjective hosannah.

Ultimate affronts to
Human redundancies;

Non-esteem of self-styled "his betters"
Leading, as he well knew,
To his final
Exclusion from the world of letters.

IV

SCATTERED Moluccas
  Not knowing, day to day,
    The first day's end, in the next noon;
The placid water
Unbroken by the Simoon;

Thick foliage
Placid beneath warm suns,
Tawn fore-shores
Washed in the cobalt of oblivions;

Or through dawn-mist
The grey and rose
Of the juridical
Flamingoes;

A consciousness disjunct,
Being but this overblotted
Series
Of intermittences;

Coracle of Pacific voyages,
The unforecasted beach;
Then on an oar
Read this:

"I was
And I no more exist;
Here drifted
An hedonist."

MEDALLION

LUINI in porcelain!
The grand piano
Utters a profane
Protest with her clear soprano.

The sleek head emerges
From the gold-yellow frock
As Anadyomene in the opening
Pages of Reinach.

Honey-red, closing the face-oval,
A basket-work of braids which seem as if they were
Spun in King Minos' hall
From metal, or intractable amber;

The face-oval beneath the glaze,
Bright in its suave bounding-line, as,
Beneath half-watt rays,
The eyes turn topaz.

HOMAGE
TO
SEXTUS
PROPERTIUS

(1917)

Orfeo

"Quia pauper amavi."

I

SHADES of Callimachus, Coan ghosts of
        Philetas
        It is in your grove I would walk,
I who come first from the clear font
Bringing the Grecian orgies into Italy,
                            and the dance into Italy.
Who hath taught you so subtle a measure,
                        in what hall have you heard it;
What foot beat out your time-bar,
                what water has mellowed your whistles?

Out-weariers of Apollo will, as we know, continue
        their Martian generalities,
        We have kept our erasers in order.
A new-fangled chariot follows the flower-hung
        horses;
A young Muse with young loves clustered about her
                    ascends with me into the æther, . . .
And there is no high-road to the Muses.

Annalists will continue to record Roman reputa-
        tions,
Celebrities from the Trans-Caucasus will belaud
        Roman celebrities
And expound the distentions of Empire,
But for something to read in normal circumstances?
For a few pages brought down from the forked hill
        unsullied?
I ask a wreath which will not crush my head.
                    And there is no hurry about it;
I shall have, doubtless, a boom after my funeral,
Seeing that long standing increases all things
                        regardless of quality.

And who would have known the towers
                        pulled down by a deal-wood horse;
Or of Achilles withstaying waters by Simois
Or of Hector spattering wheel-rims,
Or of Polydmantus, by Scamander, or Helenus and
    Deiphoibos?
Their door-yards would scarcely know them, or
    Paris.
Small talk O Ilion, and O Troad
                        twice taken by Oetian gods,
If Homer had not stated your case!

And I also among the later nephews of this city
                        shall have my dog's day,
With no stone upon my contemptible sepulchre;
My vote coming from the temple of Phoebus in
    Lycia, at Patara,
And in the mean time my songs will travel,
And the devirginated young ladies will enjoy them
                        when they have got over the strangeness,
For Orpheus tamed the wild beasts—
                        and held up the Threician river;
And Citharaon shook up the rocks by Thebes
        and danced them into a bulwark at his pleasure,
And you, O Polyphemus?   Did harsh Galatea
    almost
Turn to your dripping horses, because of a tune,
    under Aetna?
We must look into the matter.
Bacchus and Apollo in favour of it,
There will be a crowd of young women doing
        homage to my palaver,
Though my house is not propped up by Taenarian
        columns from Laconia (associated with Nep-
        tune and Cerberus),
Though it is not stretched upon gilded beams:

My orchards do not lie level and wide
        as the forests of Phaecia,
        the luxurious and Ionian,
Nor are my caverns stuffed stiff with a Marcian
    vintage,
My cellar does not date from Numa Pompilius,
Nor bristle with wine jars,
Nor is it equipped with a frigidaire patent;
Yet the companions of the Muses
        will keep their collective nose in my books,
And weary with historical data, they will turn to my
    dance tune.

Happy who are mentioned in my pamphlets,
        the songs shall be a fine tomb-stone over their
        beauty.
        But against this?
Neither expensive pyramids scraping the stars in
    their route,
Nor houses modelled upon that of Jove in East Elis,
Nor the monumental effigies of Mausolus,
        are a complete elucidation of death.

Flame burns, rain sinks into the cracks
And they all go to rack ruin beneath the thud of the
    years.
Stands genius a deathless adornment,
        a name not to be worn out with the years.

II

I HAD been seen in the shade, recumbent on
       cushioned Helicon,
       The water dripping from Bellerophon's horse,
Alba, your kings, and the realm your folk
              have constructed with such industry
Shall be yawned out on my lyre—with such industry.
My little mouth shall gobble in such great fountains,
"Wherefrom father Ennius, sitting before I came,
       hath drunk."

I had rehearsed the Curian brothers, and made
       remarks on the Horatian javelin
(Near Q. H. Flaccus' book-stall).
"Of" royal Aemilia, drawn on the memorial raft,
"Of" the victorious delay of Fabius, and the left-
              handed battle at Cannae,
Of lares fleeing the "Roman seat" . . .
                     I had sung of all these
And of Hannibal,
              and of Jove protected by geese.
And Phoebus looking upon me from the Castalian
       tree,
Said then "You idiot! What are you doing with
       that water:
"Who has ordered a book about heroes?
              "You need, Propertius, not think
"About acquiring that sort of a reputation.
       "Soft fields must be worn by small wheels,
"Your pamphlets will be thrown, thrown often into
       a chair
"Where a girl waits alone for her lover;
       "Why wrench your page out of its course?
"No keel will sink with your genius
       "Let another oar churn the water,
"Another wheel, the arena; mid-crowd is as bad as
       mid-sea."

He had spoken, and pointed me a place with his
    plectrum:

        Orgies of vintages, an earthern image of
            Silenus
Strengthened with rushes, Tegaean Pan,
The small birds of the Cytharean mother,
            their Punic faces dyed in the Gorgon's lake;
Nine girls, from as many countrysides
    bearing her offerings in their unhardened hands,

Such my cohort and setting.   And she bound ivy to
    his thyrsos;
Fitted song to the strings;
                        Roses twined in her hands.
And one among them looked at me with face
    offended,
Calliope:
        "Content ever to move with white swans!
"Nor will the noise of high horses lead you ever to
    battle;
"Nor will the public criers ever have your name
                        in their classic horns,
"Nor Mars shout you in the wood at Aeonium,
            Nor where Rome ruins German riches,
"Nor where the Rhine flows with barbarous blood,
            and flood carries wounded Suevi.
"Obviously crowned lovers at unknown doors,
"Night dogs, the marks of a drunken scurry,
"These are your images, and from you the sorcer-
                izing of shut-in young ladies,
"The wounding of austere men by chicane."
        Thus Mistress Calliope,
        Dabbling her hands in the fount, thus she
Stiffened our face with the backwash of Philetas the
    Coan.

III

MIDNIGHT, and a letter comes to me from our mistress:
>   Telling me to come to Tibur:

>   *At* once!!

"Bright tips reach up from twin towers,
"Anienan spring water falls into flat-spread pools."

What *is* to be done about it?
>   Shall I entrust myself to entangled shadows,
Where bold hands may do violence to my person?

Yet if I postpone my obedience
>   because of this respectable terror,
I shall be prey to lamentations worse than a noc-
    turnal assailant.
And I shall be in the wrong,
>   *and* it will last a twelve month,
For her hands have no kindness me-ward,

Nor is there anyone to whom lovers are not sacred
    at midnight
    And in the Via Sciro.
If any man would be a lover
>   he may walk on the Scythian coast,
No barbarism would go to the extent of doing him
    harm,
The moon will carry his candle,
>   the stars will point out the stumbles,
Cupid will carry lighted torches before him
>   and keep mad dogs off his ankles.
Thus all roads are perfectly safe
>   and at any hour;
Who so indecorous as to shed the pure gore of a
    suitor?!
    Cypris is his cicerone.

What if undertakers follow my track,
                    such a death is worth dying.
She would bring frankincense and wreaths to my
    tomb,
    She would sit like an ornament on my pyre.

Gods' aid, let not my bones lie in a public location
With crowds too assiduous in their crossing of it;
For thus are tombs of lovers most desecrated.

May a woody and sequestered place cover me with
    its foliage
Or may I inter beneath the hummock
                    of some as yet uncatalogued sand;
At any rate I shall not have my epitaph in a high
    road.

IV

DIFFERENCE OF OPINION WITH LYGDAMUS

TELL me the truths which you hear of our
        constant young lady,
        Lygdamus,
And may the bought yoke of a mistress lie with
            equitable weight on your shoulders;
For I am swelled up with inane pleasurabilities
          and deceived by your reference
To things which you think I would like to believe.

No messenger should come wholly empty,
         and a slave should fear plausibilities;
Much conversation is as good as having a home.
      Out with it, tell it to me, all of it, from the
        beginning,
I guzzle with outstretched ears.
Thus? She wept into uncombed hair,
                 And you saw it.
Vast waters flowed from her eyes?
            You, you Lygdamus
Saw her stretched on her bed,—
         it was no glimpse in a mirror;
No gawds on her snowy hands, no orfevrerie,
Sad garment draped on her slender arms.
Her escritoires lay shut by the bed-feet.
Sadness hung over the house, and the desolated
    female attendants
Were desolated because she had told them her
    dreams.

She was veiled in the midst of that place,
Damp woolly handkerchiefs were stuffed into her
    undryable eyes,

And a querulous noise responded to our solicitous
    reprobations.
For which things you will get a reward from me,
              Lygdamus?
To say many things is equal to having a home.
And the other woman "has not enticed me
                     by her pretty manners,
"She has caught me with herbaceous poison,
        she twiddles the spiked wheel of a rhombus,
"She stews puffed frogs, snake's bones, the moulted
    feathers of screech owls,

"She binds me with ravvles of shrouds.
             "Black spiders spin in her bed!
"Let her lovers snore at her in the morning!
              "May the gout cramp up her feet!
"Does he like me to sleep here alone,
          Lygdamus?
"Will he say nasty things at my funeral?"

And you expect me to believe this
           after twelve months of discomfort?

V

NOW if ever it is time to cleanse Helicon;
>> to lead Emathian horses afield,
> And to name over the census of my chiefs in
> the Roman camp.
If I have not the faculty, "The bare attempt would
> be praise-worthy."
"In things of similar magnitude
>> the mere will to act is sufficient."

The primitive ages sang Venus,
>> the last sings of a tumult,
And I also will sing war when this matter of a girl is
> exhausted.
I with my beak hauled ashore would proceed in a
> more stately manner,
My Muse is eager to instruct me in a new gamut, or
> gambetto,
Up, up my soul, from your lowly cantilation,
>> put on a timely vigour.

Oh august Pierides! Now for a large-mouthed
> product.
Thus:
"The Euphrates denies its protection to the Par-
>> thian and apologizes for Crassus,"
And "It is, I think, India which now gives necks to
> your triumph,"
And so forth, Augustus. "Virgin Arabia shakes in
> her inmost dwelling."
If any land shrink into a distant seacoast,
>> it is a mere postponement of your domination.
And I shall follow the camp, I shall be duly cele-
>> brated for singing the affairs of your cavalry.
May the fates watch over my day.

Yet you ask on what account I write so many love-
lyrics
And whence this soft book comes into my mouth.
Neither Calliope nor Apollo sung these things into
my ear,
My genius is no more than a girl.

If she with ivory fingers drive a tune through the
lyre,
We look at the process.
How easy the moving fingers; if hair is mussed on
her forehead,
If she goes in a gleam of Cos, in a slither of dyed
stuff,
There is a volume in the matter; if her eyelids sink
into sleep,
There are new jobs for the author;
And if she plays with me with her shirt off,
We shall construct many Iliads.
And whatever she does or says
We shall spin long yarns out of nothing.

Thus much the fates have allotted me, and if,
Maecenas,
I were able to lead heroes into armour, I would not,
Neither would I warble of Titans, nor of Ossa
spiked onto Olympus,
Nor of causeways over Pelion,
Nor of Thebes in its ancient respectability,
nor of Homer's reputation in Pergamus,
Nor of Xerxes' two-barreled kingdom, nor of
Remus and his royal family,
Nor of dignified Carthaginian characters,
Nor of Welsh mines and the profit Marus had out
of them.

I should remember Caesar's affairs . . .

> for a background,

Although Callimachus did without them,

> and without Theseus,

Without an inferno, without Achilles attended of
  gods,

Without Ixion, and without the sons of Menoetius
  and the Argo and without Jove's grave and the
  Titans.

And my ventricles do not palpitate to Caesarial *ore
  rotundos,*

Nor to the tune of the Phrygian fathers.

Sailor, of winds; a plowman, concerning his oxen;

Soldier, the enumeration of wounds; the sheep-
  feeder, of ewes;

We, in our narrow bed, turning aside from battles:

Each man where he can, wearing out the day in his
  manner.

3

It is noble to die of love, and honourable to remain

> uncuckolded for a season.

And she speaks ill of light women,

> and will not praise Homer

Because Helen's conduct is "unsuitable."

VI

WHEN, when, and whenever death closes
  our eyelids,

Moving naked over Acheron

Upon the one raft, victor and conquered together,

Marius and Jugurtha together,

> one tangle of shadows.

Caesar plots against India,
Tigris and Euphrates shall, from now on, flow at
        his bidding,
Tibet shall be full of Roman policemen,
The Parthians shall get used to our statuary
                        and acquire a Roman religion;
One raft on the veiled flood of Acheron,
            Marius and Jugurtha together.

Nor at my funeral either will there be any long trail,
                    bearing ancestral lares and images;
No trumpets filled with my emptiness,
Nor shall it be on an Atalic bed;
            The perfumed cloths shall be absent.
A small plebeian procession.
            Enough, enough and in plenty
There will be three books at my obsequies
Which I take, my not unworthy gift, to Persephone.

You will follow the bare scarified breast
Nor will you be weary of calling my name, nor too
        weary
            To place the last kiss on my lips
When the Syrian onyx is broken.

                "He who is now vacant dust
                "Was once the slave of one passion:"
Give that much inscription
                "Death why tardily come?"

You, sometimes, will lament a lost friend,
            For it is a custom:
This care for past men,

Since Adonis was gored in Idalia, and the Cytharean
Ran crying with out-spread hair,
            In vain, you call back the shade,
In vain, Cynthia.   Vain call to unanswering shadow,
            Small talk comes from small bones.

VII

ME happy, night, night full of brightness;
Oh couch made happy by my long delec-
tations;
How many words talked out with abundant candles;
Struggles when the lights were taken away;
Now with bared breasts she wrestled against me,
Tunic spread in delay;
And she then opening my eyelids fallen in sleep,
Her lips upon them; and it was her mouth saying:
Sluggard!

In how many varied embraces, our changing arms,
Her kisses, how many, lingering on my lips.
"Turn not Venus into a blinded motion,
Eyes are the guides of love,
Paris took Helen naked coming from the bed of
Menelaus,
Endymion's naked body, bright bait for Diana,"
—such at least is the story.

While our fates twine together, sate we our eyes
with love;
For long night comes upon you
and a day when no day returns.
Let the gods lay chains upon us
so that no day shall unbind them.

Fool who would set a term to love's madness,
For the sun shall drive with black horses,
earth shall bring wheat from barley,
The flood shall move toward the fountain
Ere love know moderations,
The fish shall swim in dry streams.
No, now while it may be, let not the fruit of life
cease.

Dry wreaths drop their petals,
   their stalks are woven in baskets,
To-day we take the great breath of lovers,
   to-morrow fate shuts us in.

Though you give all your kisses
     you give but few.

Nor can I shift my pains to other,
   Hers will I be dead,
If she confer such nights upon me,
   long is my life, long in years,
If she give me many,
   God am I for the time.

VIII

JOVE, be merciful to that unfortunate woman
   Or an ornamental death will be held to
   your debit,
 The time is come, the air heaves in torridity,
The dry earth pants against the canicular heat,
But this heat is not the root of the matter:
   She did not respect all the gods;
Such derelictions have destroyed other young ladies
  aforetime,
And what they swore in the cupboard
    wind and wave scattered away.

Was Venus exacerbated by the existence of a com-
  parable equal?
   Is the ornamental goddess full of envy?
Have you contempted Juno's Pelasgian temples,
  Have you denied Pallas good eyes?

Or is it my tongue that wrongs you
                with perpetual ascription of graces?
There comes, it seems, and at any rate
        through perils, (so many) and of a vexed life,
The gentler hour of an ultimate day.

Io mooed the first years with averted head,
                And now drinks Nile water like a god,
Ino in her young days fled pellmell out of Thebes,
                Andromeda was offered to a sea-serpent
                        and respectably married to Perseus,
Callisto, disguised as a bear,
                wandered through the Arcadian prairies
                While a black veil was over her stars,
What if your fates are accelerated,
                        your quiet hour put forward,
You may find interment pleasing,

You will say that you succumbed to a danger
        identical,
                charmingly identical, with Semele's,
And believe it, and she also will believe it,
                        being expert from experience,
And amid all the gloried and storied beauties of
        Maeonia
There shall be none in a better seat, not
                        one denying your prestige,

Now you may bear fate's stroke unperturbed,
Or Jove, harsh as he is, may turn aside your ultimate
        day.
Old lecher, let not Juno get wind of the matter,
Or perhaps Juno herself will go under,
                        If the young lady is taken?

There will be, in any case, a stir on Olympus.

IX

THE twisted rhombs ceased their clamour of
    accompaniment;
    The scorched laurel lay in the fire-dust;
The moon still declined to descend out of heaven,

But the black ominous owl hoot was audible.

And one raft bears our fates
                on the veiled lake toward Avernus
Sails spread on Cerulean waters, I would shed tears
    for two;
I shall live, if she continue in life,
        If she dies, I shall go with her.
Great Zeus, save the woman,
        or she will sit before your feet in a veil,
        and tell out the long list of her troubles.

2

Persephone and Dis, Dis, have mercy upon her,
There are enough women in hell,
             quite enough beautiful women,
Iope, and Tyro, and Pasiphae, and the formal girls
    of Achaia,
And out of Troad, and from the Campania,
Death has his tooth in the lot,
           Avernus lusts for the lot of them,
Beauty is not eternal, no man has perennial fortune,
Slow foot, or swift foot, death delays but for a
    season.

My light, light of my eyes,

                    you are escaped from great peril,

Go back to Great Dian's dances bearing suitable
    gifts,

Pay up your vow of night watches

                    to Dian goddess of virgins,

And unto me also pay debt:

The ten nights of your company you have

                  promised me.

X

LIGHT, light of my eyes, at an exceeding late
      hour I was wandering,

  And intoxicated,

               and no servant was leading me,

And a minute crowd of small boys came from op-
    posite,

                I do not know what boys,

And I am afraid of numerical estimate,

And some of them shook little torches,

               and others held onto arrows,

And the rest laid their chains upon me,

          and they were naked, the lot of them,

And one of the lot was given to lust.

"That incensed female has consigned him to our
    pleasure."

So spoke. And the noose was over my neck.

And another said "Get him plumb in the middle!

      "Shove along there, shove along!"

And another broke in upon this:

        "He thinks that we are not gods."

"And she has been waiting for the scoundrel,
                and in a new Sidonian night cap,
And with more than Arabian odours,
                God knows where he has been.
She could scarcely keep her eyes open
                enter that much for his bail.
                Get along now!"

We were coming near to the house,
                and they gave another yank to my cloak,
And it was morning, and I wanted to see if she was
    alone, and resting,
And Cynthia was alone in her bed.
                I was stupefied.
I had never seen her looking so beautiful,
                No, not when she was tunick'd in purple.

Such aspect was presented to me, me recently
    emerged from my visions,
You will observe that pure form has its value.

"You are a very early inspector of mistresses.
"Do you think I have adopted your habits?"
            There were upon the bed no signs of a
                voluptuous encounter,
            No signs of a second incumbent.

She continued:
            "No incubus has crushed his body against
                me,
            "Though spirits are celebrated for adul-
                tery.
            "And I am going to the temple of
                Vesta . . . "
                and so on.

Since that day I have had no pleasant nights.

XI

1

THE harsh acts of your levity!
                    Many and many.
I am hung here, a scare-crow for lovers.

2

Escape! There is, O Idiot, no escape,
        Flee if you like into Ranaus,
                    desire will follow you thither,
Though you heave into the air upon the gilded
        Pegasean back,
Though you had the feathery sandals of Perseus
To lift you up through split air,
The high tracks of Hermes would not afford you
        shelter.

Amor stands upon you, Love drives upon lovers,
                    a heavy mass on free necks.

It is our eyes you flee, not the city,
You do nothing, you plot inane schemes against me,
Languidly you stretch out the snare
                    with which I am already familiar,

And yet again, and newly rumour strikes on my ears.

Rumours of you throughout the city,
                    and no good rumour among them.

"You should not believe hostile tongues.
        "Beauty is slander's cock-shy.
"All lovely women have known this,"
        "Your glory is not outblotted by venom,"
"Phoebus our witness, your hands are unspotted."

A foreign lover brought down Helen's kingdom
            and she was led back, living, home;
The Cytharean brought low by Mars' lechery
            reigns in respectable heavens, . . .

Oh, oh, and enough of this,
            by dew-spread caverns,
The Muses clinging to the mossy ridges;
            to the ledge of the rocks:
Zeus' clever rapes, in the old days,
            combusted Semele's, of Io strayed.
Oh how the bird flew from Trojan rafters,
Ida has lain with a shepherd, she has slept between
    sheep.

            Even there, no escape
Not the Hyrcanian seaboard, not in seeking the
    shore of Eos.

All things are forgiven for one night of your
    games. . . .
Though you walk in the Via Sacra, with a peacock's
    tail for a fan.

XII

WHO, who will be the next man to entrust his
            girl to a friend?
    Love interferes with fidelities;
The gods have brought shame on their relatives;
Each man wants the pomegranate for himself;
Amiable and harmonious people are pushed incon-
    tinent into duels,
A Trojan and adulterous person came to Menelaus
    under the rites of hospitium,

And there was a case in Colchis, Jason and that
　　woman in Colchis;
And besides, Lynceus,

　　　　　　you were drunk.

Could you endure such promiscuity?
　　　　　　She was not renowned for fidelity;
But to jab a knife in my vitals, to have passed on a
　　swig of poison,
Preferable, my dear boy, my dear Lynceus,
Comrade, comrade of my life, of my purse, of my
　　person;
But in one bed, in one bed alone, my dear Lynceus
　　　I deprecate your attendance;
I would ask a like boon of Jove.

And you write of Achelöus, who contended with
　　Hercules,
You write of Adrastus' horses and the funeral rites
　　of Achenor,
And you will not leave off imitating Aeschylus.
　　　　Though you make a hash of Antimachus,
You think you are going to do Homer.
　　　　And still a girl scorns the gods,
Of all these young women
　　　not one has enquired the cause of the world,
Nor the modus of lunar eclipses
　　　　Nor whether there be any patch left of us
After we cross the infernal ripples,
　　　nor if the thunder fall from predestination;
Nor anything else of importance.

Upon the Actian marshes Virgil is Phoebus' chief of
　　police,
　　　　He can tabulate Caesar's great ships.
He thrills to Ilian arms,
　　　　He shakes the Trojan weapons of Aeneas,
And casts stores on Lavinian beaches.

Make way, ye Roman authors,
                    clear the street, O ye Greeks,
For a much larger Iliad is in the course of construc-
    tion
(and to Imperial order)
Clear the streets, O ye Greeks!

And you also follow him "neath Phrygian pine
    shade:
            Thyrsis and Daphnis upon whittled reeds,
And how ten sins can corrupt young maidens;
            Kids for a bribe and pressed udders,
Happy selling poor loves for cheap apples.

Tityrus might have sung the same vixen;
            Corydon tempted Alexis,
Head farmers do likewise, and lying weary amid
    their oats
They get praise from tolerant Hamadryads."
Go on, to Ascraeus' prescription, the ancient,
                    respected, Wordsworthian:
"A flat field for rushes, grapes grow on the slope."

And behold me, small fortune left in my house.
Me, who had no general for a grandfather!
I shall triumph among young ladies of indeter-
    minate character,
My talent acclaimed in their banquets,
            I shall be honoured with yesterday's
                wreaths.
And the god strikes to the marrow.

            Like a trained and performing tortoise,
I would make verse in your fashion, if she should
    command it,

With her husband asking a remission of sentence,
>> And even this infamy would not attract
>> numerous readers
Were there an erudite or violent passion,
For the nobleness of the populace brooks nothing
>> below its own altitude.
One must have resonance, resonance and sonority
>> . . . like a goose.

Varro sang Jason's expedition,
>> Varro, of his great passion Leucadia,
There is song in the parchment; Catullus the highly
>> indecorous,
Of Lesbia, known above Helen;
And in the dyed pages of Calvus,
>> Calvus mourning Quintilia,
And but now Gallus had sung of Lycoris.
>> Fair, fairest Lycoris—
The waters of Styx poured over the wound:
And now Propertius of Cynthia, taking his stand
>> among these.

CANTUS PLANUS

THE black panther lies under his rose tree
And the fawns come to sniff at his sides:

Evoe, Evoe, Evoe Baccho, O
ZAGREUS, *Zagreus*, Zagreus,

The black panther lies under his rose tree.

|| Hesper adest.   Hesper || adest.
Hesper || adest. ||

APPENDIX I

EARLY POEMS, NOT PREVIOUSLY COLLECTED, AND NOW
ADDED TO THIS COLLECTION IN 1949, INCLUDING
THE POEMS OF T. E. HULME.

TO WHISTLER, AMERICAN

On the loan exhibit of his paintings at the Tate Gallery.

YOU also, our first great,
  Had tried all ways;
  Tested and pried and worked in many fashions,
And this much gives me heart to play the game.

Here is a part that's slight, and part gone wrong,
And much of little moment, and some few
Perfect as Dürer!
"In the Studio" and these two portraits,[1] if I had my
    choice!
And then these sketches in the mood of Greece?

You had your searches, your uncertainties,
And this is good to know—for us, I mean,
Who bear the brunt of our America
And try to wrench her impulse into art.

You were not always sure, not always set
To hiding night or tuning "symphonies";
Had not one style from birth, but tried and pried
And stretched and tampered with the media.

You and Abe Lincoln from that mass of dolts
Show us there's chance at least of winning through.

[1] "Brown and Gold—de Race."
"Grenat et Or—Le Petit Cardinal."

(*Poetry, 1912*)

MIDDLE-AGED

"'TIS but a vague, invarious delight
As gold that rains about some buried
king.

As the fine flakes,
When tourists frolicking
Stamp on his roof or in the glazing light
Try photographs, wolf down their ale and cakes
And start to inspect some further pyramid;

As the fine dust, in the hid cell
Beneath their transitory step and merriment,
Drifts through the air, and the sarcophagus
Gains yet another crust
Of useless riches for the occupant,
So I, the fires that lit once dreams
Now over and spent,
Lie dead within four walls
And so now love
Rains down and so enriches some stiff case,
And strews a mind with precious metaphors,

And so the space
Of my still consciousness
Is full of gilded snow,

The which, no cat has eyes enough
To see the brightness of."

(*Poetry, 1912*)

ABU SALAMMAMM—
A SONG OF EMPIRE

Being the sort of poem I would write if King George V should have
me chained to the fountain before Buckingham Palace, and should
give me all the food and women I wanted.
To my brother in chains Bonga-Bonga.

GREAT is King George the Fifth,
      for he has chained me to this fountain;
    He feeds me with beef-bones and wine.
Great is King George the Fifth—
His palace is white like marble,
His palace has ninety-eight windows,
His palace is like a cube cut in thirds,
It is he who has slain the Dragon
        and released the maiden Andromeda.
Great is King George the Fifth;
For his army is legion,
His army is a thousand and forty-eight soldiers
        with red cloths about their buttocks,
And they have red faces like bricks.
Great is the King of England and greatly to be feared,
For he has chained me to this fountain;
He provides me with women and drinks.
Great is King George the Fifth
        and very resplendent is this fountain.
It is adorned with young gods riding upon dolphins
And its waters are white like silk.
Great and Lofty is this fountain;
And seated upon it is the late Queen, Victoria,
The Mother of the great king, in a hoop-skirt,
   Like a woman heavy with child.

Oh may the king live forever!
Oh may the king live for a thousand years!
For the young prince is foolish and headstrong;
He plagues me with jibes and sticks,

And when he comes into power
He will undoubtedly chain someone else to this foun-
tain,
And my glory will
Be at an end.

(Poetry, 1914)

L'HOMME MOYEN SENSUEL [1]

"I hate a dumpy woman"
—*George Gordon, Lord Byron.*

'TIS of my country that I would endite,
In hope to set some misconceptions right.
My country?   I love it well, and those good
fellows
Who, since their wit's unknown, escape the gallows.
But you stuffed coats who're neither tepid nor dis-
tinctly boreal,
Pimping, conceited, placid, editorial,
Could I but speak as 'twere in the "Restoration"
I would articulate your perdamnation.
This year perforce I must with circumspection—
For Mencken states somewhere, in this connection:
"It is a moral nation we infest."
Despite such reins and checks I'll do my best,

[1] (*Note:* It is through no fault of my own that this diversion was
not given to the reader two years ago; but the commercial said it
would not add to their transcendent popularity, and the vers-libre
fanatics pointed out that I had used a form of terminal consonance
no longer permitted, and my admirers (j'en ai), ever nobly desirous
of erecting me into a sort of national institution, declared the work
"unworthy" of my mordant and serious genius. So a couple of the
old gentlemen are dead in the interim, and, alas, two of the great
men mentioned in passing, and the reader will have to accept the
opusculus for what it is, some rhymes written in 1915. I would give
them now with dedication "To the Anonymous Compatriot Who
Produced the Poem 'Fanny,' Somewhere About 1820," if this form
of centennial homage be permitted me. It was no small thing to have
written, in America, at that distant date, a poem of over forty pages
which one can still read without labour. *E.P.*) [*The Little Re-
view, 1917*]

An art! You all respect the arts, from that infant
    tick
Who's now the editor of *The Atlantic,*
From Comstock's self, down to the meanest resident,
Till up again, right up, we reach the president,
Who shows his taste in his ambassadors:
A novelist, a publisher, to pay old scores,
A novelist, a publisher and a preacher,
That's sent to Holland, a most particular feature,
Henry Van Dyke, who thinks to charm the Muse you
    pack her in
A sort of stinking deliquescent saccharine.
The constitution of our land, O Socrates,
Was made to incubate such mediocrities,
These and a taste in books that's grown perennial
And antedates the Philadelphia centennial.
Still I'd respect you more if you could bury
Mabie, and Lyman Abbot and George Woodberry,
For minds so wholly founded upon quotations
Are not the best of pulse for infant nations.
Dulness herself, that abject spirit, chortles
To see your forty self-baptized immortals,
And holds her sides where swelling laughter cracks
    'em
Before the "Ars Poetica" of Hiram Maxim.
All one can say of this refining medium
Is "Zut! Cinque lettres!" a banished gallic idiom,
Their doddering ignorance is waxed so notable
'Tis time that it was capped with something quotable.

Here Radway grew, the fruit of pantosocracy,
The very fairest flower of their gynocracy.
Radway? My hero, for it will be more inspiring
If I set forth a bawdy plot like Byron
Than if I treat the nation as a whole.
Radway grew up. These forces shaped his soul;

These, and yet God, and Dr. Parkhurst's god, the
    N. Y. *Journal*
(Which pays him more per week than The Supernal).
These and another godlet of that day, your day
(You feed a hen on grease, perhaps she'll lay
The sterile egg that is still eatable:
"Prolific Noyes" with output undefeatable).
From these he (Radway) learnt, from provosts and
    from editors unyielding
And innocent of Stendhal, Flaubert, Maupassant and
    Fielding.
They set their mind (it's still in that condition)—
May we repeat; the Centennial Exposition
At Philadelphia, 1876?
What it knew then, it knows, and there it sticks.
And yet another, a "charming man," "sweet nature,"
    but was Gilder,
De mortuis verum, truly the master builder?

From these he learnt. Poe, Whitman, Whistler,
    men, their recognition
Was got abroad, what better luck do you wish 'em,
When writing well has not yet been forgiven
In Boston, to Henry James, the greatest whom we've
    seen living.
And timorous love of the innocuous
Brought from Gt. Britain and dumped down a'top of
    us,
Till you may take your choice: to feel the edge of
    satire or
Read Bennett or some other flaccid flatterer.
Despite it all, despite your Red Bloods, febrile con-
    cupiscence
Whose blubbering yowls you take for passion's es-
    sence;
Despite it all, your compound predilection

For ignorance, its growth and its protection
(Vide the tariff), I will hang simple facts
Upon a tale, to combat other tracts,
"Message to Garcia," Mosher's propagandas
That are the nation's botts, collicks and glanders.
Or from the feats of Sumner cull it?   Think,
Could Freud or Jung unfathom such a sink?

My hero, Radway, I have named, in truth,
Some forces among those which "formed" his youth:
These heavy weights, these dodgers and these
        preachers,
Crusaders, lecturers and secret lechers,
Who wrought about his "soul" their stale infection.
These are the high-brows, and to this collection
The social itch, the almost, all but, not quite, fasci-
        nating,
Piquante, delicious, luscious, captivating:
Puffed satin, and silk stockings, where the knee
Clings to the skirt in strict (vide: *"Vogue"*) pro-
        priety.
Three thousand chorus girls and all unkissed,
O state sans song, sans home-grown wine, sans real-
        ist!
"Tell me not in mournful wish-wash
Life's a sort of sugared dish-wash!"
Radway had read the various evening papers
And yearned to imitate the Waldorf capers
As held before him in that unsullied mirror
The daily press, and monthlies nine cents dearer.
They held the very marrow of the ideals
That fed his spirit; were his mental meals.
Also, he'd read of christian virtues in
That canting rag called *Everybody's Magazine,*
And heard a clergy that tries on more wheezes
Than e'er were heard of by Our Lord Ch .... J ....

So he "faced life" with rather mixed intentions,
He had attended country Christian Endeavour Con-
 ventions,
Where one gets more chances
Than Spanish ladies had in old romances.
(Let him rebuke who ne'er has known the pure Pla-
 tonic grapple,
Or hugged two girls at once behind a chapel.)
Such practices diluted rural boredom
Though some approved of them, and some deplored
 'em.
Such was he when he got his mother's letter
And would not think a thing that could upset
 her. . . .
Yet saw an "ad." "To-night, THE HUDSON
 SAIL,
With forty queens, and music to regale
The select company: beauties you all would know
By name, if named." So it was phrased, or rather
 somewhat so
I have mislaid the "ad.," but note the touch,
Note, reader, note the sentimental touch:
His mother's birthday gift. (How pitiful
That only sentimental stuff will sell!)

Yet Radway went. A circumspectious prig!
And then that woman like a guinea-pig
Accosted, that's the word, accosted him,
Thereon the amorous calor slightly frosted him.
(I burn, I freeze, I sweat, said the fair Greek,
I speak in contradictions, so to speak.)

I've told his training, he was never bashful,
And his pockets by ma's aid, that night with cash full,
The invitation had no need of fine aesthetic,
Nor did disgust prove such a strong emetic
That we, with Masefield's vein, in the next sentence

Record "Odd's blood! Ouch! Ouch!" a prayer,
 his swift repentance.

No, no, they danced. The music grew much louder
As he inhaled the still fumes of rice-powder.
Then there came other nights, came slow but cer-
 tain
And were such nights that we should "draw the cur-
 tain"
In writing fiction on uncertain chances
Of publication; "Circumstances,"
As the editor of *The Century* says in print,
"Compel a certain silence and restraint."
Still we will bring our "fiction as near to fact" as
The Sunday school brings virtues into practice.

Soon our hero could manage once a week,
Not that his pay had risen, and no leak
Was found in his employer's cash. He learned the
 lay of cheaper places,
And then Radway began to go the paces:
A rosy path, a sort of vernal ingress,
And Truth should here be careful of her thin dress—
Though males of seventy, who fear truths naked
 harm us,
Must think Truth looks as they do in wool pyjamas.
(My country, I've said your morals and your
 thoughts are stale ones,
But surely the worst of your old-women are the male
 ones.)

Why paint these days? An insurance inspector
For fires and odd risks, could in this sector
Furnish more date for a compilation
Than I can from this distant land and station,
Unless perhaps I should have recourse to
One of those firm-faced inspecting women, who

Find pretty Irish girls in Chinese laundries,
Upstairs, the third floor up, and have such quandaries
As to how and why and whereby they got in
And for what earthly reason they remain. . . .
Alas, eheu, one question that sorely vexes
The serious social folk is "just what sex is."
Though it will, of course, pass off with social science
In which their mentors place such wide reliance.
De Gourmont says that fifty grunts are all that will be prized.
Of language, by men wholly socialized,
With signs as many, that shall represent 'em
When thoroughly socialized printers want to print 'em.
"As free of mobs as kings"?   I'd have men free of that invidious,
Lurking, serpentine, amphibious and insidious
Power that compels 'em
To be so much alike that every dog that smells 'em,
Thinks one identity is
Smeared o'er the lot in equal quantities.
Still we look toward the day when man, with unction,
Will long only to be a *social function*,
And even Zeus' wild lightning fear to strike
Lest it should fail to treat all men alike.
And I can hear an old man saying: "Oh, the rub!
"I see them sitting in the Harvard Club,
"And rate 'em up at just so much per head,
"Know what they think, and just what books they've read,
"Till I have viewed straw hats and their habitual clothing
"All the same style, same cut, with perfect loathing."

So Radway walked, quite like the other men,
Out into the crepuscular half-light, now and then;

Saw what the city offered, cast an eye
Upon Manhattan's gorgeous panoply,
The flood of limbs upon Eighth Avenue
To beat Prague, Budapesht, Vienna or Moscow,[1]
Such animal invigorating carriage
As nothing can restrain or much disparage. . . .
Still he was not given up to brute enjoyment,
An anxious sentiment was his employment,
For memory of the first warm night still cast a haze
 o'er
The mind of Radway, whene'er he found a pair of
 purple stays or
Some other quaint reminder of the occasion
That first made him believe in immoral suasion.
A temperate man, a thin potationist, each day
A silent hunter off the Great White Way,
He read *The Century* and thought it nice
To be not too well known in haunts of vice—
The prominent haunts, where one might recognize
 him,
And in his daily walks duly capsize him.
Thus he eschewed the bright red-walled cafés and
Was never one of whom one speaks as "brazen'd."

Some men will live as prudes in their own village
And make the tour abroad for their wild tillage—
I knew a tourist agent, one whose art is
To run such tours.   He calls 'em. . . . house par-
 ties.
But Radway was a patriot whose venality
Was purer in its love of one locality,
A home-industrious worker to perfection,
A senatorial jobber for protection,
Especially on books, lest knowledge break in
Upon the national brains and set 'em achin'.
('Tis an anomaly in our large land of freedom,

---

[1] Pronounce like respectable Russians: "*Mussqu.*"

You can not get cheap books, even if you need 'em).
Radway was ignorant as an editor,
And, heavenly, holy gods! I can't say more,
Though I know one, a very base detractor,
Who has the phrase "As ignorant as an actor."

But turn to Radway: the first night on the river,
Running so close to "hell" it sends a shiver
Down Rodyheaver's prophylactic spine,
Let me return to this bold theme of mine,
Of Radway. O clap hand ye moralists!
And meditate upon the Lord's conquests.
When last I met him, he was a pillar in
An organization for the suppression of sin. . . .
Not that he'd changed his tastes, nor yet his habits,
(Such changes don't occur in men, or rabbits).
Not that he was a saint, nor was top-loftical
In spiritual aspirations, but he found it profitable,
For as Ben Franklin said, with such urbanity:
"Nothing will pay thee, friend, like Christianity."
And in our day thus saith the Evangelist:
"Tent preachin' is the kind that pays the best."

'Twas as a business asset *pure an' simple*
That Radway joined the Baptist Broadway Temple.

I find no moral for a peroration,
He is the prototype of half the nation.

PIERROTS

From the French of Jules Laforgue
(Scene courte mais typique)

YOUR eyes!   Since I lost their incandescence
Flat calm engulphs my jibs,
The shudder of *Vae soli* gurgles beneath my
ribs.

You should have seen me after the affray,
I rushed about in the most agitated way
Crying: My God, my God, what will she say?!

My soul's antennæ are prey to such perturbations,
Wounded by your indirectness in these situations
And your bundle of mundane complications.

Your eyes put me up to it.
I thought: Yes, divine, these eyes, but what exists
Behind them?   What's there?   Her soul's an af-
fair for oculists.

And I am sliced with loyal æsthetics.
Hate tremolos and national frenetics.
In brief, violet is the ground tone of my phonetics.

I am not "that chap there" nor yet "The Superb"
But my soul, the sort which harsh sounds disturb,
Is, at bottom, distinguished and fresh as a March
herb.

My nerves still register the sounds of contra-bass',
I can walk about without fidgeting when people pass,
Without smirking into a pocket-looking-glass.

Yes, I have rubbed shoulders and knocked off my
chips
Outside your set but, having kept faith in your eyes,
You might pardon such slips.

247

Eh, make it up?

Soothings, confessions;

These new concessions

Hurl me into such a mass of divergent impressions.

(The Little Review, 1917)

DONNA MI PREGA

(*Dedicace*—To Thomas Campion his ghost, and to the ghost of
Henry Lawes, as prayer for the revival of music)

BECAUSE a lady asks me, I would tell
Of an affect that comes often and is fell
And is so overweening: Love by name.
E'en its deniers can now hear the truth,
I for the nonce to them that know it call,
Having no hope at all

that man who is base in heart
Can bear his part of wit

into the light of it,
And save they know't aright from nature's source
I have no will to prove Love's course

or say
Where he takes rest; who maketh him to be;
Or what his active *virtu* is, or what his force;
Nay, nor his very essence or his mode;
What his placation; why he is in verb,
Or if a man have might

To show him visible to men's sight.

In memory's locus taketh he his state   *Place*
Formed there in manner as a mist of light   *La ove*
Upon a dusk that is come from Mars and stays. *chilo*
Love is created, hath a sensate name,   *fa*
His modus takes from soul, from heart his will; *creare*
From form seen doth he start, that, understood,
Taketh in latent intellect—

248

As in a subject ready—
                    place and abode,
Yet in that place it ever is unstill,
Spreading its rays, it tendeth never down
By quality, but is its own effect unendingly
Not to delight, but in an ardour of thought
That the base likeness of it kindleth not.

It is not *virtu,* but perfection's source   *VIRTÙ*
Lying within perfection postulate   *e*
Not by the reason, but 'tis felt, I say.   *potenza*
Beyond salvation, holdeth its judging force,
Maintains intention reason's peer and mate;
Poor in discernment, being thus weakness' friend,
Often his power meeteth with death in the end
Be he withstayed
                    or from true course
                                        bewrayed
E'en though he meet not with hate
                                    or villeiny
Save that perfection fails, be it but a little;
Nor can man say he hath his life by chance
Or that he hath not stablished seigniory
Or loseth power, e'en lost to memory.
He comes to be and is when will's so great   *Essenza*
It twists itself from out all natural measure;   *e*
Leisure's adornment puts he then never on,   *movimento*
Never thereafter, but moves changing state,
Moves changing colour, or to laugh or weep
Or wries the face with fear and little stays,
Yea, resteth little
                    yet is found the most
Where folk of worth be host.
And his strange property sets sighs to move
And wills man look into unformed space
Rousing there thirst
                    that breaketh into flame.

None can imagine love
                        that knows not love;
Love doth not move, but draweth all to him;
Nor doth he turn
                for a whim
                                to find delight
Nor to seek out, surely,
                        great knowledge or slight.

Look drawn from like,   *Piacimento*
                delight maketh certain in seeming
Nor can in covert cower,
                        beauty so near,
Not yet wild-cruel as darts,
So hath man craft from fear
                                in such his desire
To follow a noble spirit,
                edge, that is, and point to the dart,
Though from her face indiscernible;
He, caught, falleth
                plumb the spike of the targe.
Who well proceedeth, form not seeth,
                following his own emanation.
There, beyond colour, essence set apart,
In midst of darkness light light giveth forth
Beyond all falsity, worthy of faith, alone
That in him solely is compassion born.

Safe may'st thou go my canzon whither thee pleaseth
Thou art so fair attired that every man and each
Shall praise thy speech
So he have sense or glow with reason's fire,
To stand with other
                hast thou no desire.

(*Make It New, 1935*)

250

THE COMPLETE POETICAL
WORKS OF T. E. HULME [1]

PREFATORY NOTE

In publishing his *Complete Poetical Works* at thirty,[2] Mr Hulme has set an enviable example to many of his contemporaries who have had less to say.

They are reprinted here for good fellowship; for good custom, a custom out of Tuscany and of Provence; and thirdly, for convenience, seeing their smallness of bulk; and for good memory, seeing that they recall certain evenings and meetings of two years gone, dull enough at the time, but rather pleasant to look back upon.

As for the "School of Images," which may or may not have existed, its principles were not so interesting as those of the "inherent dynamists" or of *Les Unanimistes,* yet they were probably sounder than those of a certain French school which attempted to dispense with verbs altogether; or of the Impressionists who brought forth:

"Pink pigs blossoming upon the hillside";

or of the Post-Impressionists who beseech their ladies to let down slate-blue hair over their raspberry-coloured flanks.

Ardoise rimed richly—ah, richly and rarely rimed! —with *framboise.*

As for the future, *Les Imagistes,* the descendants of the forgotten school of 1909, have that in their keeping.

I refrain from publishing my proposed *Historical Memoir* of their forerunners, because Mr Hulme has threatened to print the original propaganda.

E.P.

---

[1] First published at the end of the volume *Ripostes* in 1912
[2] Mr Pound has grossly exaggerated my age.—T.E.H.

AUTUMN

A TOUCH of cold in the Autumn night—
    I walked abroad,
        And saw the ruddy moon lean over a hedge
Like a red-faced farmer.
I did not stop to speak, but nodded,
And round about were the wistful stars
With white faces like town children.

MANA ABODA

Beauty is the marking-time, the stationary vi-
bration, the feigned ecstasy of an arrested im-
pulse unable to reach its natural end.

M ANA ABODA, whose bent form
    The sky in archèd circle is,
        Seems ever for an unknown grief to mourn.
Yet on a day I heard her cry:
"I weary of the roses and the singing poets—
Josephs all, not tall enough to try."

ABOVE THE DOCK

A BOVE the quiet dock in mid night,
    Tangled in the tall mast's corded height,
        Hangs the moon.   What seemed so far away
Is but a child's balloon, forgotten after play.

THE EMBANKMENT

(The fantasia of a fallen gentleman on a
cold, bitter night.)

ONCE, in finesse of fiddles found I ecstasy,
In the flash of gold heels on the hard pave-
ment.
Now see I
That warmth's the very stuff of poesy.
Oh, God, make small
The old star-eaten blanket of the sky,
That I may fold it round me and in comfort lie.

CONVERSION

LIGHTHEARTED I walked into the valley
wood
In the time of hyacinths,
Till beauty like a scented cloth
Cast over, stifled me.   I was bound
Motionless and faint of breath
By loveliness that is her own eunuch.
Now pass I to the final river
Ignominiously, in a sack, without sound,
As any peeping Turk to the Bosphorus.

APPENDIX II

VERSE OF THE THIRTIES, FIRST PRINTED IN *THE NEW ENGLISH WEEKLY*, AND ADDED TO THIS COLLECTION IN 1949. (PROSE BY A. R. ORAGE.)

POEMS OF ALFRED VENISON
The Poet of Titchfield Street

THE CHARGE OF THE
BREAD BRIGADE

HALF a loaf, half a loaf,
Half a loaf?   Um-hum?
Down through the vale of gloom
Slouched the ten million,
Onward th' 'ungry blokes,
Crackin' their smutty jokes!
We'll send 'em mouchin' 'ome,
Damn the ten million!

There goes the night brigade,
They got no steady trade,
Several old so'jers know
Monty has blunder'd.
Theirs not to reason why,
Theirs but to buy the pie,
Slouching and mouching,
Lousy ten million!

Plenty to right of 'em,
Plenty to left of 'em,
Yes, wot is left of 'em,
Damn the ten million.
Stormed at by press and all,
How shall we dress 'em all?
Glooming and mouching!

See 'em go slouching there,
With cowed and crouching air
Dundering dullards!
How the whole nation shook
While Milord Beaverbrook
Fed 'em with hogwash!

ALF'S SECOND BIT

Sir,—Your printing of my little piece about the Hunger Marchers has encouraged me to send you another. They come to me while I'm pushing my rabbit-barrow down Titchfield Street. I don't claim to be as educated as some of your other poets; but I attend night schools and pick up a bit of the dictionary that way. It would tickle my missus to see this new bit in print.

A.V.

THE NEO-COMMUNE

MANHOOD of England,
  Dought of the Shires,
    Want Russia to save 'em
And answer their prayers.
Want Russia to save 'em,
Lenin to save 'em, Trotsky to save 'em
(And valets to shave 'em)
The youth of the Shires!

Down there in Cambridge
Between auction and plain bridge,
  Romance, revolution 1918!
An idea between 'em
I says! 'ave you seen 'em?
The flower of Cambridge,
The youth of the Shires?

ALF'S THIRD BIT

Sir,—Lumme, I was pleased, and so was the missus, to see my bit in your paper last week. Any luck this time?

A.V.

DOLE THE BELL! BELL THE DOLE!

WHOM can these duds attack?
  Soapy Sime? Slipp'ry Mac?
    Naught but a shirt is there
Such as the fascists wear,
Never the man inside

Moving a nation-wide
   Disgust with hokum.

Plenty to right of 'em,
Plenty to left of 'em,
Yeh!   What is left of 'em,
   Boozy, uncertain.
See how they take it all,
Down there in Clerkenwall
Readin' th' pypers!

Syrup and soothing dope,
Sure, they can live on hope,
   Ain't yeh got precedent?
Ten years and twelve years gone,
Ten more and nothing done,
   GOD save Britannia!

ALF'S FOURTH BIT

Sir,—That looked to me all right last week, though I didn't think
you'd print my letter as well.   How's this?

A.V.

R UDYARD the dud yard,
   Rudyard the false measure,
   Told 'em that glory
Ain't always a pleasure,
But said it wuz glorious nevertheless
To lick the boots of the bloke
That makes the worst mess.

Keep up the grand system
Don't tell what you know,
Your grandad got the rough edge.
Ain't it always been so?

Your own ma' warn't no better
Than the Duchess of Kaugh.
My cousin's named Baldwin
An' 'e looks like a toff.

You 'ark to the sargent,
And don't read no books;
Go to God like a sojer;
What counts is the looks.

ALF'S FIFTH BIT

Sir,—I've tried a bit of fancy-work this time; and I hope to see it
in print like the rest.

A.V.

THE pomps of butchery, financial power,
Told 'em to die in war, and then to save,
Then cut their saving to the half or lower;
When will this system lie down in its grave?

The pomps of Fleet St., festering year on year,
Hid truth and lied, and lied and hid the facts.
The pimps of Whitehall ever more in fear,
Hid health statistics, dodged the Labour Acts.

All drew their pay, and as the pay grew less,
The money rotten and more rotten yet,
Hid more statistics, more feared to confess
C.3, C.4, 'twere better to forget

How many weak of mind, how much tuberculosis
Filled the back alleys and the back to back houses.
"The medical report this week discloses . . ."
"Time for that question!"   Front Bench interposes.

Time for that question? and the time is NOW.
Who ate the profits, and who locked 'em in

The unsafe safe, wherein all rots, and no man can say
    how
What was the nation's, now by Norman's kin
Is one day blown up large, the next, sucked in?

ALF'S SIXTH BIT

*Sir,—I've put the names in, but you can leave them out if they're
friends of yours. It's what I think.*

                                                    A.V.

LET some new lying ass,
    Who knows not what is or was,
        Talk economics,
Pay for his witless noise,
Get the kid nice new toys,
    Call him "professor."

Lies from the specialist
Give t'old ones a newer twist
    Harder to untie.
Here comes the hired gang
Blood on each tired fang
    Covered with lip-stick.

"Oh, what a charming man,"—
That's how the press blurb ran,—
    "Professor Keynes is."
Now they can't fire him.
NO! they won't hire him.
    Still Dr. Soddy's
Not tied to the ring around,
Not quite snowed under.
    Being a physicist
They can't quite bribe him.
Oh, what a noise they made
    Those parliamentarians.

Oh what a fuss they made
Stirring the marmalade
    These parliamentarians
Never an honest word
In their dim halls was heard
    For more than a decade.

ALF'S SEVENTH BIT

Sir,—If the Co-ops want my address, you can give it to them. I
guess they ought to be grateful to you and me for showing up the
game.

                                                                A.V.

DID I 'ear it 'arf in a doze:
    The Co-ops was a goin' somewhere,
    Did I 'ear it while pickin' 'ops;
How they better start takin' care,

That the papers were gettin' together
And the larger stores were likewise
Considering something that would, as you
Might say, be a surprise

To the Co-ops, a echo or somethin'?
They tell me that branded goods
Don't get a discount like Mr. Selfridge
Of 25 per cent. on their ads., and the woods

Is where the Co-ops are goin' to,
And that Oxford Street site
Is not suited to co-operation—
A sort of Arab's dream in the night.

"We have plenty, so let it be."
The example of these consumers in co-
        operation
Might cause thought and be therefore
A peril to Selfridge and the nation.

ALF'S EIGHTH BIT

Sir,—I've been reading some of the other fellers' poetry lately;
and, lumme, if I don't think I can do it as well as any of them; and
with real meat in mine, not just my own rabbits. What say you?

A.V.

VEX not thou the banker's mind
    (His *what?*) with a show of sense,
    Vex it not, Willie, his mind,
    Or pierce its pretence
On the supposition that it ever
Was other, or that this cheerful giver
Will give, save to the blind.

Come not anear the dark-browed sophist
    Who on the so well-paid ground
Will cheerfully tell you a fist is no fist,
    Come not here
With 2 and 2 making 4 in reason,
Knowest thou not the truth is never in season
    In these quarters or Fleet St.?

In his eye there is death,—I mean the banker's,—
    In his purse there is deceit,
It is he who buys gold-braid for the swankers
    And gives you Australian iced rabbits' meat
In place of the roast beef of Britain,
And leaves you a park bench to sit on
    If you git off the Embankment.

This is the kind of tone and solemnity
    That used to be used on the young,
My old man got no indemnity
    But he swaller'd his tongue.
Like all his class was told to hold it in those days,
To mind their "p's" and their "q's" and their ways
An' be thankful for occasional holidays.

I don't quite see the joke any more,
   Or why we should stand to attention
And lick the dirt off the floor
   In the hope of honourable mention
From a great employer like Selfridge
Or a buyer of space in the papers.
I'm getting too old for such capers.

ALF'S NINTH BIT

Sir,—Here's another improvement on a worn-out model. I did it
very nearly in my sleep. A bit of genius, what?

A.V.

LISTEN, my children, and you shall hear
   The midnight activities of Whats-his Name,
      Scarcely a general now known to fame
Can tell you of that famous day and year.

When feeble Mr. Asquith, getting old,
The destinies of England were almost sold
To a Welsh shifter with an ogling eye,
And Whats-his-name attained nobility.

The Dashing Rupert of the pulping trade,
Rough from the virgin forests inviolate,
Thus rose in Albion, and tickled the State
And where he once set foot, right there he stayed.

Old 'Erb was doting, so the rumour ran,
And Rupert ran the rumour round in wheels,
And David's harp let out heart-rending squeals:
"Find us a harpist!! DAVID is the man!!"

Dave was the man to sell the shot and shell,
And Basil was the Greek that rode around
On sea and land, with all convenience found
To sell, to sell, to sell, that's it, to SELL

Destroyers, bombs and spitting mitrailleuses.
He used to lunch with Balfour in those days
And if the papers seldom sang his praise,
The simple Britons never knew he was,

Until a narsty German told them so.
Listen, my children, and you shall hear
Of things that happened very long ago,
And scarcely heed one word of what you hear.

Bury it all, bury it all well deep,
And let the blighters start it all over again.
They'll trick you again and again, as you sleep;
But you shall know that these were the men.

ALF'S TENTH BIT

Sir,—Seems to me that at this rate I shall have written enough
to make a book before long. But I'm beginning to be guessed in
Titchfield Street; and a lady asked me the other day if I sold veni-
son! Is this what they call fame?

A.V.

WIND

SCARCE and thin, scarce and thin
    The government's excuse,
  Never at all will they do
Aught of the slightest use.
Over the dying half-wits blow,
Over the empty-headed, and the slow
    Marchers, not getting for'arder,
While Ramsay MacDonald sleeps, sleeps.

Fester and rot, fester and rot,
    And angle and tergiversate
One thing among all things you will not
    Do, that is: *think,* before it's too late.
Election will not come very soon,

And those born with a silver spoon,
  Will keep it a little longer,
Until the mind of the old nation gets a little **stronger.**

ALF'S ELEVENTH BIT

Sir,—I've had a go this week at the big bugs; and don't I know
'em! My little kid is one of their victims, and a proper mess they'd
make of him if I didn't watch out.

A.V.

SIR LAUNCELOT HAS A
NEWSPAPER NOW

MY great press cleaves the guts of men,
  My great noise drowns their cries,
  My sales beat all the other ten,
Because I print most lies.

I get the kids out on the street
To sell the papers early,
At one o'clock I go to lunch,
Looking so big and burly.

I wear a fine fur coat and gloves,
And spats above my shoes,
They have to do the dirty work,
I do whatever I choose.

They have to stand about in mud
And cold fit for despair,
But I have made a ruddy pile
From profits on hot air.

I pump the market up and down
By rigging stock reports,
And get my pickings on the side
From dress goods ads, and sports.

The King was once the biggest thing
In England?   I'll say YES!
But knights and Lords to-day respect
The power of the Press.

ALF'S TWELFTH BIT

Sir,—Can I bring rabbits out of the hat as well as off my barrow?
Watch me! How's this for the rabbit in Mr. Montague's hat?
Didn't know it was there, did he?

A.V.

BALLAD FOR THE *TIMES'*
SPECIAL SILVER NUMBER

S EZ the *Times* a silver lining
  Is what has set us pining,
                    Montague, Montague!

In the season sad and weary
When our minds are very bleary,
                    Montague, Montague!

There is Sir Hen. Deterding
His phrases interlarding,
                    Montague, Montague!

With the this and that and what
For putting silver on the spot,
                    Montague, Montague!

Just drop it in the slot
And it will surely boil the pot,
                    Montague, Montague!

Gold, of course, is solid too,
But some silver set to stew
                    Might do, too.   Montague!

With a lively wood-pulp "ad."
To cheer the bad and sad,
                    Montague, Montague!

ANOTHER BIT—
AND AN OFFER

Sir,—I reckon the apparatus is punctured, what with the Budget
and all. With your kind permish, I'll make my tens of thousands
of readers a sporting offer. The first that sends you £10 shall have
the twelve poems dedicated to him and printed in a book to sell off
my barrer with the rabbits. And you, kind Sir, will see fair play
as between patron and poet. Now, then, who's going to be the
lucky first?

I SEE by the morning papers
   That America's sturdy sons
   Have started a investigation
Of the making of guns.

The morning paper tells me
They have asked the senate to guess
Whether Mr. Dupont and the gun-sharks
Have influence with the press.

I sit alone in the twilight
After my work is done
And wonder if my day's three and eight-pence
Would count on the price of a gun.

Was I started wrong as a kiddie,
And would my old man have been smarter
To send me to work in Vickers
Instead of being a carter?

                                    A.V.

SAFE AND SOUND

MY name is Nunty Cormorant
And my finance is sound,
I lend you Englishmen hot air
At one and three the pound.

I lend you Englishmen hot air
And I get all the beef
While you stalwart sheep of freedom
Are on the poor relief.

Wot oh! my buxom hearties,
What ain't got work no more
And don't know what bug is a-bitin'
To keep your feelin's sore,

There is blokes in automobiles
And their necks sunk into fur
That keep on gettin' usury
To make 'em cosier.

I read these fellers puts it
Most tidily away
And then lends out their printed slips
To keep the wolf away

From their vaults and combination
Safes in Thread and Needle street.
I wouldn't 'ave the needle
If I had more grub to eat.

Oh the needle is your portion,
My sufferin' fellow men,
Till the King shall take the notion
To own his coin again.

A.V.

SONG OF SIX HUNDRED M.P.'S

"WE are 'ere met together
in this momentous hower,
Ter lick th' bankers' dirty boots
an' keep the Bank in power.

We are 'ere met together
ter grind the same old axes
And keep the people in its place
a'payin' us the taxes.

We are six hundred beefy men
(but mostly gas and suet)
An' every year we meet to let
some other feller do it.

I see their 'igh 'ats on the seats
an' them sprawling on the benches
And thinks about a Rowton 'ouse
and a lot of small street stenches.

"O Britain, muvver of parliaments,
'ave you seen yer larst sweet litter?
Could yeh swap th' brains of orl this lot
fer 'arft a pint o' bitter?"

"I couldn't," she sez, "an' I aint tried,
They're me own," she sez to me,
"As footlin' a lot as was ever spawned
to defend democracy."

A.V.

OLE KATE

W HEN I was only a youngster,
   Sing: toodle doodlede oot!
   Ole Kate would git her 'arf a pint
And wouldn't giv' a damn hoot.

"Them stairs! them stairs, them gordam stairs
Will be the death of me."
I never heerd her say nothin'
About the priv'lege of liberty.

She'd come a sweatin' up with the coals
An a-sloshin' round with 'er mop,
Startin' in about 6 a.m.
And didn't seem never to stop.

She died on the job they tells me,
Fell plump into her pail.
Never got properly tanked as I saw,
And never got took to jail,

Just went on a sloshin'
And totin' up scuttles of coal,
And kissin' her cat fer diversion,
God rest her sloshin' soul.

"Gimme a kissy-cuddle"
She'd say to her tibby-cat,
But she never made no mention
Of this here proletariat.

                    A.V.

THE BABY

THE baby new to earth and sky
    Has never until now
      Unto himself the question put
Or asked us if the cow

Is higher in the mental scale
Than men like me and you,
Or if the cow refrains from food
Till she finds work to do.

"The baby new to earth and sky,"
As Tennyson has written,
Just goes ahead and sucks a teat
Like to-day's great men in Britain.

               A.V.

NATIONAL SONG (E.C.)

THERE is no land like England
    Where banks rise day by day,
      There are no banks like English banks
To make the people pay.

There is no such land of castles
Where an Englishman is free
To read his smutty literature
With muffins at his tea.

Chorus:

For the French have comic papers—
Not that nice Britons read 'em,
But the bawdy little Britons
Have bank sharks to bleed 'em

And to keep an eye on their readin' matter
Lest they should overhear the distressing chatter

Of the new economical theories
And ask inconvenient queeries.

(*The New English Weekly, 1932*)

END OF VENISON POEMS

NOTE.—the prose passages in the Venison sequence
(the letters preceding each poem and signed *A.V.*)
were written by A. R. Orage.

M. POM-POM

(Caf' Conc' song
The Fifth, or Permanent International)

M. Pom-POM allait en guerre
           Per vendere cannoni
      Mon beau grand frère
Ne peut plus voir
                Per vendere cannoni.

M. Pom-POM est au senat
                Per vendere cannoni
Pour vendre des canons
Pour vendre des canons
                To sell the god damn'd frogs
                A few more canon.

(*Townsman, 1938*)

INDEX OF TITLES
AND FIRST LINES